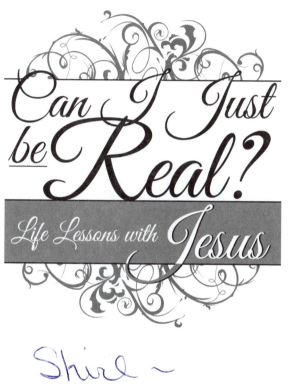

Shirl ~

Blessings to you

Aleasa

Life Lessons with Jesus

by Leesa L. Shultz

Can I Just be Real? Life Lessons with Jesus
Copyright © 2017 Leesa L. Shultz. All rights reserved

All scripture quoted from Zondervan NIV Study Bible, Holy Bible, New International Version unless otherwise noted. Copyright 1973, 1978, 1984 by International Bible Society. Used by permission of Zondervan. All rights reserved.

Published by: Fire Wheat LLC www.firewheat.com
Fire Wheat ™ is a trademark of Fire Wheat LLC, Rochester, MN

Christian Living, Religion & Spirituality, Spiritual Warfare, Inspirational, Christian Faith, Christian Spiritual Growth, Christian Women's Issues, Prayer

Published in the United States of America

Graphic Design created by Nick Sinclair

Cover photo: Stock photo ID:472251602 • misfire_asia

Edited by Jen Vick, Becke Rieck, Lizabeth Shultz, Betsy Miller, Rebecca Atwood

Project Manager-Rose Korabek

Author Photo by Missy Talmadge

ISBN: 978-0-9982721-3-9

Endorsements

"*Can I Just be Real* has it all. Leesa has written a book that delivers smiles and thought-provoking insights page after page. With grace, humility, transparency and wit, Leesa shares her life and relationship with Jesus in a way that is relatable and inspiring. *Can I Just be Real* is a fantastic work that deals head on with the struggles many women face. With a fast-moving narrative and quick wit this book does an amazing job bringing to life Mary and Martha from the pages of the Bible. These two ladies go from honorable-mention with a footnote to real-life women with personality quirks, dreams, ambitions, and struggles. It doesn't take long to realize that several thousand years may separate Mary and Martha from the women of today, but the struggles are still the same. Insanely practical and insightful, *Can I Just be Real* is sure to encourage women in any stage of their lives. After reading this book you will never look at Mary and Martha the same way, and more importantly, you will never see yourself the same."
 —**Ryan Hawley,** *Author and Senior Pastor of Prince of Peace Christian Church, Tomahawk, WI*

"Every woman is wonderfully made and is designed to be adored by their Daddy. Leesa Shultz brings forth a very down-to-earth approach, bringing women closer to the adoration of their Heavenly Father. She meticulously brings you closer to the mirror that reflects His image of you."
 —**Steven Wilson,** *Author of Fire Wheat for Entrepreneurs, and Teacher*

"In a world of so much polish and Pinterest, I find myself having to off-road to discover the experiences of God-loving women that are gritty and interesting. In *Can I Just be Real* Leesa gets raw and relatable to show us how a messy curiosity about the ways of God can turn us into hearty women and passionate daughters of a good Father. If you're through with just 'doing devotions' and are ready to be devoted to Jesus with all of your crazy, scuffed-up life, Leesa's candid conversations will draw you in to the deeper things of everyday discipleship."

–Tahni Cullen, speaker and author of Josiah's Fire: Autism Stole His Words, God Gave Him a Voice

Acknowledgements

As I sat down to begin this journey, it was the Holy Spirit and me in the room: me at the typewriter, and Him whispering over my shoulder. He was the true writer, and I was the scribe. If the Holy Spirit spoke, I typed. If the Holy Spirit didn't speak, I didn't type. So, of course, all credit goes to Him. It was never my intention to write a book, but it would appear He knew this would be more than just my ramblings on a laptop. It was the Lord, Jesus, and the Holy Spirit tugging at my heart strings and encouraging me to open that door to my heart which I have guarded so desperately and to give you a peek inside. It hasn't been easy and at times quite painful as I, yet again, took a tour of duty to the past. But, as you will learn, sweet healing comes daily for me, as it will for you.

There are so many dear friends and family that have joined me on this adventure and I want each of you to know that this book is from you and for you.

Steve Wilson, this book would not be more than a hope and a dream if not for you investing and believing in me. You are a man of integrity in every sense of the word, and your commitment to the Kingdom advancement and unity of the body is amazing! You model Jesus as a man who has spent much time with Him.

Wednesday ladies, this book was inspired by you. As I watched you worship and seek the Lord with every ounce of your being, I couldn't help but have to share your passion with others. You inspired me to share what true intimacy with Jesus really looks like. So Sandy, Deb, Aja, Marian, Lucy, Jane, Amy, Rose, Betsy, Alivia, and others who have passed through, bless you. You ladies are the kind of warriors I wish every woman could encounter. You are not afraid to be real and vulnerable, and that seems to melt the heart of God and bring Him so near. That is what it's all about – being real! You are prayer warriors, watchmen, intercessors, truth tellers, and women who are madly in love with Jesus. You are amazing!

"My girls" – some of you by birth and some of you by heart – what do I do with you? Becke, Liz, Amy and Linda (dear sister), you have inspired me, pushed me, encouraged me relentlessly, believed in me, loved me, laughed and cried with me and for me, read and re-read this manuscript, spent endless hours compensating for my pitiful computer skills, dreaming with me, interceding for me, and lifting me up when I really wanted to stay in bed and pull the covers over my head until Jesus came back.

Bill, you have been a patient husband. You are a man of few words, but when words come they are filled with wisdom and common sense. You are my rock in every sense of the word, physically and spiritually, and I know that no matter what crazy thing I come up with, or when my impulsive nature flares up, you will always have my back. There are times when I have thrown you under the bus and times when I have left you standing alone, and yet, like Jesus, you never, ever leave me nor forsake me. Thank you for your quiet, steadfast, solid nature.

Jake, I love that you curl up on the chair with me as I type, and I love your sweet puppy snuggles. You are my little buddy and faithful companion. I appreciate the endless hours you have spent keeping my lap warm while I was busy creating.

Contents

Foreword 15
1 Heart to Heart 19
2 Let's Get Real 33
3 Balmy Breezes & Babbling Brooks 39
4 The Slippery Slope 45
5 Warrior Heart 51
6 What Did You Say? 57
7 Crisis of Faith 65
8 Fire Walkers 71
9 The Narrow Road 81
10 Milk or Meat? 89
11 Talk is Cheap 99
12 Life is Messy, Get Used to it 105
13 Lay it Down 113
14 Potato Fights & Squirt Guns 121
15 One Last Cup of Tea 129
Epilogue 131
Who You Are In Christ 135
Prayer of Authority 141
Endnotes 143

Foreword

Can I be real with you? If we are going to spend the next few hours or days or weeks together, I want to be as transparent as possible. This book is about taking a journey together, learning what it looks like to sit at the feet of Jesus, and being still in the midst of this crazy world. I have examined the story of Martha and Mary from many angles in this book, and what I hope you will take from it more than anything else is what every woman longs to hear; Jesus just wants your heart! Sit down, take a load off, and relax. Nobody cares, except you, if your laundry hasn't been folded in days, and your meals aren't going to win any awards from Martha Stewart. (Well, your husband may care about this one, but he will just have to chill.)

Martha was a Type A personality all the way. If you want things to get done and float all your ducks in a row in the same pond, you want a Type A on your team. Being Type A can be a great asset; however, no matter who we are, deep, true intimacy demands we learn the art of listening more than we speak. We also need to learn to be content in the solitude of our prayer closet. Stop trying to strive for the "perfect" status. As Martha realized, sometimes it is necessary to take off the apron, put the china away, stop polishing the silver, and get out the paper napkins. Just order pizza, grab the disposable plates and sit down at Jesus' feet and relax.

I, too, have had to learn these lessons the hard way. Have you ever sat down and turned the hallowed pages of *Redbook, Cosmopolitan,* or *Martha Stewart Living* and felt totally inept? A good day for me is just getting out of bed without spraining anything, throwing some bread in the toaster, fetching two-day-old wrinkled clothes from the dryer, and hoping like crazy the mirror won't show any more wrinkles that decided to make an appearance overnight. So, now that you have a peek into my glamorous life, please don't envy me. Let's sit down with the Guest of Honor and just breathe in His sweet presence.

In this book you will often hear me refer to the Lord as "Daddy." I know there are some who might be offended at what seems a lack of reverence. I do not mean this to be. Many times in scripture, Jesus called His Father "Abba," which in Aramaic would most closely be translated as "Daddy." I have the utmost respect and awe for our Heavenly Father. "In the council of the holy ones God is greatly feared; he is more awesome than all who surround him," Psalm 89:7.

However, He is also my heavenly Father who is pleased to be my "Daddy." As a child, my earthly father didn't know how to be a daddy to a little girl with wounds. He loved me and I knew it, but he didn't know how to show it. God loves me unconditionally and He knows how to show it. He filled my lonely heart, healed my wounds, and in every sense of the word is a Daddy to me. I respect Him as God the creator, but I also know Him as a Daddy who welcomes me to come to Him as a little child. "I tell you the truth, unless you change and become like little children, you will never enter the kingdom of heaven." Matthew 18:2.

I want to make one disclaimer. I have chosen not to capitalize the name of satan. It is my personal preference and not a grammatical error. My entire life has been a battle to overcome and walk in freedom from the target satan put on me before I was even born. In Christ, I have overcome. I have been set free. I am a child of the Most High God. I REFUSE to give satan credit in any way!

As Jesus and his disciples were on their way, he came to a village where a woman named Martha opened her home to him. She had a sister called Mary, who sat at the Lord's feet listening to what he said. But Martha was distracted by all the preparations that had to be made. She came to him and asked, "Lord, don't you care that my sister has left me to do the work by myself? Tell her to help me!"

"'Martha, Martha,' the Lord answered. 'You are worried and upset about many things, but only one thing is needed. Mary has chosen what is better, and it will not be taken away from her.'"

Luke 10:38-42
Zondervan NIV Study Bible

1
Heart to Heart

God has an interesting sense of timing. A few days ago this chapter was not even a thought. The book was in its final stages of editing and preparing for the cover graphics, and I was looking forward to seeing a printed copy within a month or so. I was excited to be coming to a close and seeing the finished product. I love to laugh, and I wanted this book to have humor mixed with the heaviness that it carries in places. I wanted you to be able to relate to my crazy side that loves to laugh, especially at myself. However, I'm afraid this first chapter might hit you hard and heavy. Please bear with me as we get through it. I promise it gets lighter.

Less than a week ago the Lord said to me that there is one more chapter, and it is going to be the first one. It entails a heart-to-heart conversation we had just had, and I had no intention of sharing it with anyone except Him and me. It was an honest conversation that was raw and vulnerable. Remember, this book is all about being real and I am certainly being real here. I didn't intend for it to be this early in the book but it's God's book, so He gets to write it!

Early one morning I sat down with a cup of tea and my journal and asked God to show me His heart. I had been struggling with lots of emotions and questions, and I needed answers. Part of my struggle in sharing this is that it is very personal for me. The other part is that I have trouble believing that anyone would be interested in hearing me talk about me! But I'm going to share this because the Lord asked me to do it. This is a raw and revealing introduction about the journey of my intimacy with Jesus that we will be talking about in this book. It has taken me many, many years and much pain to get to this level of intimacy with the Lord; an intimacy where I can share my heart with Him and I know He will share His with me.

I have to share a bit about my childhood in order for my conversation with the Lord to make sense. He gave me straight-up answers to my questions. I didn't hold back and neither did He. I am completely overwhelmed and undone at His kindness and compassion for humanity.

I was born with severe asthma. I am told that I would frequently stop breathing and my parents would have to rush me to the emergency room at a very nearby hospital. After many times of this, the doctor told my parents to treat me at home. This involved plunging my lifeless, blue body into a sink of ice water to shock my body into breathing on its own again. Ironically, both of my parents chain smoked, so this didn't help my already weak lungs. At three years of age I fell down a set of basement steps and broke my collarbone. The rest of my childhood was a haze of infections, strep throats, ear infections, and a blur of hospital stays. As a teenager, many mornings I would wake up only to find that my mother had been taken to the hospital because of one of the many illnesses that began to plague her. My dad later contracted emphysema because of his heavy smoking. If you know anything about trauma and its effects on our spiritual being, this is trauma! Trauma is when something bad happens to us beyond our control. This allows an open door for the enemy to speak his lies to us. He uses it as a gateway to our soul.

I will share later about my experiences with day care and the trauma that was inflicted there. My parents both worked, and as soon as I was able to stay home alone I was relieved to be able to do so. My brother and sister were quite a bit older than me, graduated and away from home while I was still young. During the summer when there was no school, the days became very long and lonely. We lived five miles from the nearest town, and neighbors were few and far between.

My days were spent walking in the woods and through meadows with my only friends – my dog and an army of cats. The dog and cats were my constant companions. I spent hours and hours on lonely summer days playing and talking with them. There was also a stream behind our barn that I would dangle my toes in for hours as I imagined what it would be like to have friends and siblings with whom to play.

My life has been plagued with illness since that time as an infant. As an adult, I juggled raising two small children, a new marriage, and all the baggage that comes with that. In addition, we had my very ill father live with us in our tiny house. At one point when he was in the hospital, my mother informed him she wanted a divorce, so we invited him to live with us. He later suffered a heart attack on my kitchen floor as my two-year-old and ten-month-old children watched. He passed away after a ten-day hospital stay.

Shortly after that, my mother became ill and experienced kidney failure. For the next ten years she would be in and out of hospitals. She had to go on dialysis, and the nearest facility was eighty miles away. Three times a week I would get my pre-school children up at 5:00 a.m., take them to a babysitter, and go with my mother to receive her treatments. It didn't matter if there was a blizzard or tornado. We HAD to go! If we went in the ditch, which we did, we had to get pulled out and keep going. She eventually received a kidney transplant but suffered years of complications. She was in and out of hospitals with heart failures, surgeries, and illnesses that ravaged her body. More than once the family was called to come because she wasn't expected to live. Twice my sister and I had to fly to Texas, where she spent the winters, to say "goodbye." Each time she pulled through. But, eventually her frail body gave out. I sat with her as her organs failed and she said goodbye to this world. More trauma was taking its toll on me.

During this time, I believe because of stress, my own body began to fail me as well. I had unbearable migraine headaches for years. I had my ovaries removed, one at a time, because of extremely painful cysts. My gall bladder was removed due to severe pain, from which I still suffer. I have had bouts of depression, one of which rendered me totally unable to function. For an entire year I laid on my couch staring into space, paralyzed by this ugliness. Just when I thought I might get a break I was diagnosed with a thyroid issue which fluctuated from *hypo*thyroid to *hyper*thyroid like a yoyo. I had part of my thyroid surgically removed. Then years later the other half had to be destroyed by radioactivity. Imagine being in a lab with a nurse wearing lead gloves up to her elbows, a mask, and vest. She hands you a lead canister, with another canister inside, with a little pill that she dumps in your bare hand and says, "Swallow this."

Years later, I am still fluctuating and it throws my hormones off like crazy. I have poor circulation in my hands and feet, and most of the time they are literally like little ice cubes. There's more! I now have undiagnosed stomach pain. The latest treatment has been to limit myself to a diet of applesauce and bananas. If I eat anything else I will double over in pain. This has been going on for weeks, and I have lost over fifteen pounds. (There is always a silver lining.) And last, but certainly not least, I have anxiety so severe that I haven't made the hour and half trip to see my daughter in almost a year. Is any of this screaming trauma?

So, obviously, I had some questions for my Daddy. I have heard all the theological answers and I am familiar with Job. But I just needed a heart-to-heart. Some of this conversation you may or may not believe or agree with. I am not trying to convince you of anything or any doctrine. I am sharing this because the Lord asked me to. If any of it resonates with you or helps you through your own "dark night of the soul" then please be blessed. If not, feel free to go to the next chapter.

Some of my questions may seem shocking, but remember, this book is about a journey into intimacy. My journey has been a long one. It has taken time to get to the point that I can ask such intimate questions and know that as long as I ask with a pure heart, my Father will answer with honesty. So here we are. I asked, and He answered.

"Lord, what is wrong with me? I was just at the doctor again and am having more tests done. Please be honest with me. What is your will in this? Are you a man, Lord, that you would violate your covenant?

"This is what your word says to me, 'Blessed is he who has regard for the weak; the Lord delivers him in times of trouble. The Lord will protect him and preserve his life; he will bless him in the land and not surrender him to the desire of his foes. The Lord will sustain him on his sickbed and restore him from his bed of illness. I said, O Lord, have mercy on me for I have sinned against you,' Psalm 41. 'Lord, do you violate your covenant or alter what your lips have uttered?' Psalm 89:4.

"This is your word, straight from scripture. You will heal me from my sickbed. Father, I ache to be whole to fulfill my destiny from you with strength and joy. Restore life to me. Your word says you will restore me (many, many times). Will you give me a stone or a snake? Will you say you will heal and restore me and yet leave me lying in my sick bed? Are you a man that you will deny your child healing? Have I not trusted you? In my pain I have cried to you. In my loneliness I have cried to you. Father have you turned your back on me? Have I grieved you? Lord, allow me this question. I have been sick my whole life. Will it always be this way until you take me home?"

"No, child, you will be whole."

"What must I do to be healed? I have taken authority over all generational iniquities. Lord, you know how hard I have fought. What am I missing? Why do you overlook me? Why does my body betray me? I need to really know your heart."

"Sweet child, I have spoken My destiny over you. That destiny will be fulfilled. Age means nothing to Me. Your journey has not been wasted."

"Lord, tell me about my illnesses. Why have I been so sick my whole life? Am I not made whole in you? Will this continue without end? It wearies me. Why do I miss out on so much? There has been so much loneliness. Why do I have to live with so much fear and anxiety? What purpose does it serve? It is not of you. It does not glorify you. It is ugly."

"My child, all are conceived to this earthly home for a chosen time and a chosen purpose. You were chosen before time began to be a warrior. You were conceived in strife. The generations before you were rebellious and stiff-necked. But you were not an accident, you were chosen. Even in the womb of your mother you had to fight for life. Satan knew you well even at conception. He saw the mark of the warrior upon your brow even then. Enmity has always been between you and him. At birth as you drew your first breath he purposed in his heart that it would be your last. If not for My hand on you, it would have been. At night he would stand over your infant body and suck air from your tiny lungs. Even then you had to fight. He purposed if he couldn't steal your life, he would inflict trauma. Many times he would steal your breath and each time I would breathe my life back into your body.

"In ignorance, your parents knew not how to care for you. Much trauma was inflicted upon your innocent soul. Doctors misdiagnosed and mistreated you. You were plunged into ice water as your cold, blue body fought for its every breath. I was there, and I wept over you."

"But Father you have authority over satan. Why didn't you make him stop?"

"You were given from my hands into the hands of your earthly parents. You came to earth at your chosen time to fulfill a destiny agreed upon before the earth was formed. To be a warrior in my kingdom is a great honor. Only the greatest of warriors endure the many scars inflicted. It is what makes them warriors. As the lonely child you were, satan could have taken your life many times. I would not allow it. I saw your loneliness. I was there. Satan tried many times to lure you away from Me. He enticed you to study witchcraft. He enticed you, out of loneliness, into unhealthy friendships.

"I loved your parents. I longed for them to love me and walk in my ways. I trusted my child into their care. I knew they would fail you, but I loved them and never stopped calling to them. Child, at conception your six angels were assigned to you. (The ones I showed you years ago). They will usher you into my presence when it is time. Until that time they surround you. They surrounded you as you struggled for air and they surround you as you fight for peace."

Years ago I received a vision from the Lord. I was standing with six angels encircling me, who were about ten feet tall. They had their backs to me and I was in the center. Their enormous wings were spread shoulder to shoulder and the wing tips were like razor blades. I saw demons running at them only to be bloodied by the sharp razor tips. They kept trying to get past the angels and get to me but the razor-sharp edges stopped them. I then saw myself standing in the center with their backs facing me. The back of their wings bent toward me to touch my face. I physically felt the wings as they touched me. I have no word that could come close to describing the softness of those wings as they brushed against me. I just sobbed and sobbed as they caressed my face.

"Father, why do you still allow satan to steal health? Jesus secured my healing on the cross. Shouldn't I be free now?"

"Yes. The enemy can do nothing without my permission. I have allowed illness to come against you. Not to harm you but to make you strong. If your life had been easy you would not have the warrior heart you now have. Your passion burns within your heart for others from whom satan has stolen. With each sickness you have become more dependent on me. Your resolve to help others has become stronger and stronger. You have learned how to overcome so that you can teach others. Even when you strayed, My hand was ever on you."

"Lord, I don't mean to complain but I'm weary of being sick. I love you and I trust you, and I love our intimacy. But do I have to choose one over the other? Can I not be healthy and strong? Will I always have to fight so hard? How can I help others when I am lying in bed sick?"

"Child, remember when you used to play in the woods by your home? Remember the fields where you would lay and watch the clouds? You were innocent. I took great joy in watching you. Your long red hair would blow in the breeze. I would send butterflies to flutter around you. Remember the little stream that you loved? I sent cool water to tickle

your bare feet and gave you frogs who would sing just for you. Remember how they would soothe your tears with their symphonies? You loved them. I loved to bring you those small joys. You loved the smell of the fresh cut hay. I brought you kittens in every size and shape. I loved the joy they brought you. I gave them in abundance just so I could watch you play and giggle and feed them grasshoppers. I gave them freely so you wouldn't be lonely. Your tears brought pain to my heart, but it has always been my joy to redeem your tears and hear your laughter. I know the years of illness have stolen your laughter. But I will restore it. It is My promise to you.

"Your children have watched your years of suffering. It has been painful for them as well. But because you have learned to fight, they will not be under the generational curses that you were. You have leaned well. You have fought so the generations that follow you will be set free. You are strong. You have suffered much so that those who come after you will not have to. You are going after the high places and taking them down–just as I instructed Gideon to do also. Despair no more. This present illness will be overcome, and in due time, you will be even stronger. Come to Me in your weariness and lay your cares at my feet. As I have told others, at the appointed time the chains will fall off, the door will fly open, and you will be free."

"Lord, why does this anxiety plague me? Between illness and anxiety, I barely leave my house. Father, what do you want me to learn? What is your heart in this? Are you afraid I will run away and forget you if you set me free? Father I know this is wrong but I equate love with tender care. You are not powerless.

You have all power to heal and make your children whole. Hospitals are full of sick and dying children. How is this love? Please forgive me but these questions loom."

"*I receive these questions. They are from your heart. You ask why I stand by and allow suffering.*"

"Yes, Lord."

"*Where there is no hardship people forget me. Remember Joseph? His father favored and spoiled him. He felt entitled. Without hardship he was unfit to lead a nation. In comfort my people forget me and harden their hearts. A tender heart is a heart acquainted with sorrow.*"

"But why the innocent Lord?"

"*They suffer now but their reward is great. You are earthly minded, child. There is more. I am God of eternity. There is a heavenly home waiting for those who endure the momentary trials of a fallen world. Adam had dominion over your world and it was given to him in a perfect state – a replica of heaven. It was intended as my dwelling place with you in all perfection. Adam gave that dominion to satan. It was neither my intention nor my doing. Child, this is no longer your home as was intended. Yes, I could raise my hand or speak a word and bring it to an end. And, I will! I desire no one to perish, so I withhold my hand until all have had a chance to repent. Understand as best you can. Remember the Israelites. When all was well and my hand lifted all suffering, they soon forgot my kindness and went their own way. They forgot my laws, and they neglected to teach their children my precepts. Soon they became selfish and evil. In suffering, you have become teachable and humble. In my eternity, all suffering will be forgotten.*"

"So Lord, what do I do today, tomorrow, as I wait on you? I cry to You. I trust You. I sincerely need You to take my hands and guide my feet. Even my family does not fully understand my hiddenness and grow weary of it. I don't blame them. Daddy, the anxiety and constant sickness steal my joy. They weary me. I want to laugh again. I ache for times of sweet fellowship with other people. I try to be strong. I'm tired. I need Your sweet presence so badly. Please come to me. I am so grateful, Daddy, that You talk to me and with me. I am humbled that You trust me with all the questions I ask. Please show me more of Your heart. Please continue to give me hope."

"I love you. My hand is on you. The blessings you are receiving are because I trust you with stewardship. I trust you to seek My perfect will in all matters. This is only the beginning. There will be more.

"Your husband does well to receive and trust me daily. This provision is for today. Tomorrow there will be new provision. Trust your husband. He is My gift to you to take care of you. He loves you. My hand is on you as husband and wife. Your marriage has navigated stormy seas, but it has survived because My hand is upon you. It has been difficult for both of you to receive love. You were not shown how. But now you must receive My love generously.

"You see yourself coming to the end of a long, difficult road. You feel your destiny has failed. You see your age and feel your time has been wasted. You see your best years as behind you. You feel trapped by anxiety and fear. You are afraid there is nothing more for you. Sweet, sweet child, you think I see you only as a warrior. You are MY child. To you My love needs to be shown in tangible ways.

"You know I sent my Son to the cross for you. You know I love you. You just don't know how to receive it. You see your sickness as my lack of love."

"I'm sorry Father, but you are correct. I know you love me, and I love you so much. I love my time with you. Forgive me for that not being enough. It should be more than enough. Teach me, Daddy. Teach me to need you only."

"Just allow my love to be enough. I have promised you wholeness, and it will come."

"Father, only if it doesn't come at the cost of losing my intimacy with you. I don't want to be spoiled and forget you. I trust you."

I am still processing this conversation. As I said, it is raw and real. But it is only when we can be raw and real with God that we really can see His true heart. It was very difficult for me to share this chapter with you. Sharing my heart does not come easy to me. But in doing so, it is my deepest desire that you too will be real with Your Father and be real with others. Let's put away the pretense, the fake mask we wear, and stop trying to act like we are sailing through this earthly home with no scars. (Unless you really are, then Praise the Lord!!!)

Just as He promised, the Lord has been faithful. As I cried out to Him and pleaded for answers, He gave them to me. After weeks of tests, an emergency room visit, and more tests, I was led to a kind doctor who has experienced his own pain of many illnesses and has made it his business to help others. We are only in the beginning stages, but he believes I have an auto-immune disease that is attacking my body. It will mean I have to be free of gluten, wheat, dairy, soy, eggs, yeast, and sugar. I'm being real here–this is not my first choice. But, as I again went to my Father for answers, He told me that He did not create us to ingest toxins. He said our food has become so defiled that it is causing our bodies to be ravaged by disease. He told me that it is His desire for me to eat the way He created me to eat. I'm not happy about it, but I find it hard to argue. I am not a healthy person by nature, and I love my big macs and fries. And, as you will find out in a later chapter, I have a very serious sugar addiction! However, I am really sick, and if I want that to stop, I had better take my Father's advice.

In the following chapters, I share with you what my journey into intimacy looks like. Sometimes it is deep and sometimes it has humor as I laugh at myself. I have had to change the title of this book so many times that I'm not sure I will even remember it anymore. And, once again, as this non-existent chapter became Chapter One, the entire tone of the book has just been shifted. So, I invite you to dive in, and I hope you enjoy. Many of the stories are based around my observation of our sisters, Martha and Mary. They have had so much to teach me that I just had to take a deeper peek into their lives.

2

Let's Get Real

If you come to my house for a good meal served on matching plates with a lovely centerpiece, cloth napkins and nice goblets, you will be woefully disappointed. I used to be that way, but that boat has sailed. I liked putting out nice dishes on a pretty table with a ridiculous amount of food. What I didn't like was spending all my time cooking, serving, and cleaning. I would spend hours planning, fussing over the food and primping the house. Honestly, it often made me kind of ugly. I didn't look at all like I just stepped off the pages of *Martha Stewart Living*, and my guests would arrive to a hostess with bags under her eyes, hair sticking up everywhere, and longing for her bed. Eventually, I realized that I was simply not wired for "fancy." The cost of worrying about a perfect setting was costing me my sanity, and I can't afford to lose any more than I already have. I longed for something that took less preparation even if it meant sacrificing "perfect" for something more real.

It's a crazy world isn't it? We are so consumed with playing the part of a good Christian that we forget the most important things. We go to church and sit quietly in our pew. We act like we have it all together, speak out our usual answer if asked how we are ("I'm great!"), and pay our obligatory 10% (if we can afford it that week). Then we invite the pastor over for lunch and warn the kids that if they belch the alphabet in front of the pastor they can forget about leaving their room in their lifetime. We take the perfect roast out of the oven, set the best china on the table, and pray the pastor's wife doesn't notice the dust bunnies under the buffet or the water spots on the glasses. We spend our time and energy focused on how we appear, always hiding our less than perfect selves, and not letting others see the real "us."

Can I Just be Real?

Jesus was real. He loved sinners and hated hypocrisy. He didn't do fake well. He did some pretty emphatic rebuking when the Pharisees put on their prim and proper airs. Sometimes I wish I were more prim and proper, like a southern belle. I love the accent, the ladyness, the manners, and almost everything about them. They are such a great mix of cute and feisty! Unfortunately, I'm not quite in that league. I have lived in Wisconsin most of my life, I say "ain't" and "gonna," I don't drink sweet tea, and I kinda think belching the alphabet is funny. I once owned a ferret named Pedro (and laughed every time he scooted out from under the couch and scared people half to death). I'm not sure I even know how to fold a napkin into anything. Thankfully, Jesus loves us just the way we are, and we don't have to pretend to be someone we're not. But, our performance-driven society mandates such levels of unrealistic expectations, it's no wonder we're weary.

What was it about Jesus that drew Mary out of the kitchen to sit at His feet, leaving an irate Martha to do all the running around? After all, this was Jesus right there on the sofa; shouldn't she be preparing a feast to end all feasts? Shouldn't she be polishing the silver, folding the napkins into doves, basting the lamb and spiffing up the fine china? This wasn't just an ordinary guest; this was Jesus, the Son of God for goodness' sake! Only the best for Jesus! But the best we have to offer looks very different to Jesus than it does to us. He is not impressed with fancy clothes, cars, polished silver, and expensive china. Although these things are not evil, we can get so caught up in them that we forget Jesus is sitting in our living room waiting to share His heart with us. While we are busy scrubbing our valuables to impress Him, He is patiently waiting for us to just come and sit down.

Mary must have sensed this, and at the risk of her sister's wrath, she threw in her dish towel and left the kitchen. Can you just see Martha muttering to herself as she hurries around the kitchen? "The bread is burning, the potatoes are boiling over, the lamb is drying out, the silverware has water spots, the napkins aren't folded and the table isn't set. Lord have mercy, where is Mary? She's always running off, never around when you need her! This time she's gone too far… I'm marching right in there and telling Jesus the evening is ruined and it's all Mary's fault!" She enters the living room to see Mary sitting on the floor in front of the Guest of Honor, laughing at His jokes. Has she completely lost her mind? Does she expect him to eat burned lamb! "MARY!! Jesus, make her help me!" But, I can imagine Jesus, with a tender smile full of grace, may have said, "Dear Martha leave her alone. I'm not here for a fancy dinner. I'm here because I love you and want to enjoy your company. I want to know your heart and want you to know mine. Mary understands this and she has chosen what is better. Martha, join us. Let's just order pizza. Grab some paper plates. Sit down, and let's talk."

What if we followed Mary's lead? What if we put down the dishcloth and were honest with each other about how we really were doing? What if we focused more on each other's hearts and then took each other's burdens to the throne room in prayer right then and there? What if the pastor's kid belched the alphabet (gasp) and no one fainted? What might happen if we all were a little more real?

So often I've missed Jesus because I was too busy basting the lamb. How many times have you not had company over because your house was too dirty, your dishes didn't match, and you wouldn't think of serving pizza or hotdogs? When we're striving for a perfect version of ourselves, we'll find every excuse to not be real or let anyone get close to us.

One year, when the children were small, we were remodeling our tiny living room. Note the key word here is YEAR! Could it have dragged on any longer? Was this God's way of teaching me patience? If it was, I was not amused. I am not even going to talk about what I put my poor husband through. It was not my crowning glory in the pages of history! Month after month I lived with a beautiful shade of pink insulation mocking me from every wall, and plywood floors in my living room! In those days, I was a stay-at-home mom, and my only lifeline to adult conversation was having my friends over for tea parties. Any excuse was enough for me to break out the fancy tea cups and call the ladies. Sometimes we even had themes – dress up, Victorian, vintage, hats, furs, and jewels. Just come over and speak adult words to me. You know where this is going, right? Martha on steroids! But with our living room in chaos, I stopped having people over; I couldn't let them see my house like that. My pride reigned, and as the months wore on, I became lonelier and lonelier. Somewhere in the midst of this craziness I had to make some serious choices: seclusion or humility. I broke! To this day I look back at photos of tea parties, Christmas and a whole host of milestones with pink insulation smiling back at me from the walls. And guess what? It was wonderful – a unique conversation piece inciting roars of laughter. I had no choice but to lighten up and make lemonade out of those pink lemons. (However as my husband spread on the sheetrock mud, and this is the truth, I stood behind him with a hair dryer trying to get it dry enough so I could hang pictures. Yes, they had to come down, and yes, I again stood with hair dryer in hand drying freshly painted walls so they could go back up immediately.) Patience is not my strong suit. Come on now, month after long month after long month with pink walls and bare floors can take its toll on even the best of women (and I am not even in the same zip code as the best of women). Oh Martha, we are sisters at heart. I have your DNA written all over me.

Let's dare to be different! Get out the paper plates (Chinette if you really feel fancy), order pizza, and let the good times roll. Being Martha is overrated, and I want in on the real action! If Jesus ever comes to my house, he won't find me in the kitchen hand-dipping chocolate bonbons. He'll find me overdosing on someone else's hand-dipped chocolate bonbons and laughing at all of His jokes.

3

Balmy Breezes & Babbling Brooks

In northern Wisconsin, we have two seasons: frozen tundra and mosquitos. As I write, we are in the frozen tundra season. For several days, the temperature has been below zero. We have highs of -2 degrees and lows of -20 degrees, and it's still early in the season. Summer feels like a million miles away. What does one do in this paradise? If you're me, you whine a lot, but normal people just go on with business as usual. You learn to live with alligator skin and buy lotion in gallon drums. You NEVER stick your tongue on anything metal. You walk VERY carefully on ice covered sidewalks. You also have to bribe your animals to go outside long enough to relieve themselves! If you are lucky enough to have a wood stove, you plant yourself in front of it until June.

You don't know what crabby is until you've stood in a ten-foot snow drift with six layers of clothing, wind so cold your face feels like it's going to break, skin cracking, lips frozen to your teeth, enough static in your hair to power New York City for hours – and that's before you've left the front porch! Then you have to get to your car and scrape ice off the windshield and defrost all your windows just so you can go to the store and buy enough vitamin D (a.k.a. sunshine in a bottle) to get you through unending months of cloudy days and freezing temperatures. And don't tell me to "bloom where I'm planted." You know what blooms under ten feet of snow? Crabby old ladies, that's what!

From now on I'm cranking up the heat, grabbing my wool blanket and sitting at the feet of Jesus. I have my Bible and my vitamin D, and I'm not moving until June when I can once again make my way outside to be eaten alive by mosquitos (which, by the way, are the size of small birds). If you haven't figured it out yet, that's why I have gatherings at my house. These people are saints! They thank me for hosting like I was some kind of nice person. As everyone piles on their coats and hats and boots and scarves and get in freezing cars and drive home on icy roads, I simply pull my blanket over my head as I settle down on my warm couch reminiscing about what a great time we had. I'm pretty sure they have me figured out, but they still let me get away with it (for now).

Can you imagine what life was like for Eve? Before she got that apple craving, that is? I dream of myself as her walking through a field of wildflowers with balmy breezes blowing my flowing hair, playing with puppies and kittens, and no muffin top bulging over my jeans. I listen to babbling brooks; stop to smell the flowers, and enjoy breathtaking colors. Oh my dear sister Eve, I know if it hadn't been you, it would have been me reaching for that apple. But I wish it had been different. How I wish we were all still strolling in that garden talking face-to-face with our Creator. I ache for that place that He so joyfully created for us to live. What special care He took to make everything so perfect for us and how happy He was to commune with Eve face-to-face. It must have been wonderful.

This earth is not our real home anymore. It is tarnished and broken. But while I am visiting this world, I will try to see the beauty. I will still take time to smell those flowers, and play with all the puppies and kittens I can get my hands on. I will try harder to be more real than pretend. I'm so grateful that God doesn't try to hide from us. Just as in the beginning, He longs for our company, pursues us, and calls us to Him. He wants to walk side-by-side, to laugh and cry together and hang out like best friends. Have you ever had a best friend who knew everything about you and loved you anyway? You'd stay up all night at sleepovers talking, giggling, dreaming, and pondering life. I'm so grateful that we have a best friend who never sleeps! Even while we are sleeping, He is gazing at us like mothers do with their newborn babies.

Poor Martha gets a bad rap in her one little chapter of fame, but I can't help but think she had hopes and dreams and good intentions just like you and me. I don't think she wanted to be in that kitchen any more than Mary did, but she was doing what she thought was right to make her guest feel welcome. I can relate. I was just talking tonight with my Wednesday prayer ladies (I will tell you about them later), and I shared how I tend to always be observing if people seem to feel comfortable or not. It's just something most women do when they have guests in their home. I have long since stopped caring if they can write an autobiography in the dust on my coffee table, and everyone knows it wouldn't be wise to retrieve something dropped from the dinner table on the floor. But I just can't seem to stop trying to make people comfortable. Do they look chilled? Is their chair uncomfortable? Do they need water? Is the music too loud? Is the music too soft? Are they hungry? Do they like the food? Always watching, always fussing. I don't want to do it, but it sneaks up on me like the flu at one in the morning. All of a sudden it's just there! I wish I could be Mary and plop myself on the floor right there in front of Jesus and forget about everything else around me. Maybe someday I will, but for now I'm still a work in progress and I adore my friends and family who love me and accept me as I am.

God made women uniquely, and I think He smiles at the way we are so comfortable being with one another. I used to have a sectional couch, and on movie night eight to ten women would all pile on that couch, intertwining themselves into a pile of arms and legs. Someone would be braiding someone else's hair, and there was usually an assembly line of shoulder rubs and foot massages. Others were sharing their popcorn, and there was always somebody snuggling with the dog. It's just the way we are! Women are comfortable with each other. If Martha were here, we would make sure she stayed out of the kitchen. In fact, on movie nights, that's the rule: if somebody wants something they get it themselves. I can relax on movie nights and not worry about everyone else: I'm too busy getting a foot massage and snuggling the dog! Come to think of it, movie night is long overdue!

In the next chapter I'm going to share about a slippery slope leading to a place I call "the dark night of the soul." I have talked in this chapter about "living in a winter wonderland" versus strolling in the garden with Eve. I have touched on fussing and sitting. I have shared just a glimpse into the tender heart of women. We are strong yet delicate. We often love with abandon, and many of us trust easily. We understand one another, and we need the sweet fellowship we share on those "movie nights."

It's been a long road for me to get to that place where I can share my heart, both with other women and with Jesus. I tend to keep everyone at arm's length, not because I don't want to trust but because I have learned that to trust the wrong people can cause pain.

When I was three years old my family moved from a large city to a small rural area. We lived in a very run-down home several miles from the nearest town. The entire time we lived there we had a tiny bathroom that had neither a tub nor shower (sponge baths!). My earliest memories are of when I was about five years old. My parents both worked, so they would drop me off early each morning at the home of an elderly couple. I would lay down on the sofa in their living room where I was told to go back to sleep until they woke me up to have a hearty breakfast and get ready for the bus to take me to school. During the summer months I would stay all day. It should have been a time of innocence and safety. However, every morning, the husband would come into the living room and try to take off my pajamas to violate me.

At the tender age of five I learned not to trust. Every morning when I should have been safely sleeping, I was watching and waiting, as I clutched my pajamas tightly to my body. During the summer months when I was there all day, my vigilance heightened. Of course, a five-year-old doesn't understand that they have done nothing wrong. I was told never to tell, and I didn't.

To my relief, after a couple of years I was moved to the home of a wonderful farm family for daycare. I thought I could finally relax. This family had a hired man who had a trailer on the property. Quickly, I learned that trust was again elusive. He would lure me into his trailer with the promise of candy and fondle me. I was threatened not to tell, and I didn't. Surely I was doing something wrong to deserve this.

I don't remember how long this went on. I have tried to erase most memories. The foundation was laid for a heart that would not easily trust and was full of baggage that would need to be unpacked. Rebellion would follow as I got older, and a "slippery slope" beckoned to a lost and lonely young girl looking for relief from pain.

∽ 4 ∾

The Slippery Slope

I want to draw a picture for you of what happens when we carry baggage that we are never meant to carry. It's a story of how satan can separate a sheep from the fold or prey on a sheep that is not yet in the fold. It is a reminder to me that every Martha and Mary must take the hand of our lost brothers and sisters and lead them to the feet of Jesus.

"I will exalt you, O Lord, for you lifted me out of the depths and did not let my enemies gloat over me," Psalm 30:1.

The depths, or slippery slope as I call it, represent anywhere that God is not. We find ourselves trapped in the depths when we are searching for love and acceptance apart from Jesus. For some, it's a straight plummet into the depths of addiction. For others, it's a gradual decline into apathy, self-centeredness, pride, loneliness, unforgiveness, and fear. For me it was betrayal, loss of innocence, and loneliness.

Ever since the Lord had to evict our apple-eating friends and place those sword-wielding angels at the gates of the garden (Gen. 3), things have gotten a bit ugly. We are tempted and dragged into the depths of despair by our enemy. "Your enemy the devil prowls around like a roaring lion looking for someone to devour," 1 Peter 5:8. Satan hates God with such fierceness that he pours every ounce of his energy into destroying us, God's glorious creation. Unfortunately, sometimes the lying voice of the enemy is the only voice we can hear. Those lies have sucked me in at times, and I have experienced anger and jealousy. Words have come out of my mouth of which I am not proud. I have believed some of his lies, and believing those lies is what made me sink into the depths of despair and darkness. The dark, cold, murky depths are a place I've visited often. I could describe the smell, the feel, the ugliness and the loneliness.

Satan would love for us all to set up camp there and never leave. It almost makes him giddy at the thought of us pounding our tent stakes, unpacking our luggage, making our bed and digging our well. Even if we bring satin sheets and designer luggage, he is utterly satisfied. He doesn't care what we bring with us, as long as we come early and stay late. In fact, he loves all the trappings; the more the better–the cars, homes, boats, jewels, and love of money. The more comforts the better. We gorge ourselves on comforts until we are so fat on those indulgences that we feel like we do on Thanksgiving Day after eating too much turkey – tired and lazy and all too eager to stake our claim on the couch and let the chips fall where they may. It's a place where we can escape reality and pain. We just relieve our suffering with anything that will bring us a moment of pleasure. But, all too soon, we need something more to satisfy. Until we face that pain head-on, we will always be searching for something else to ease the hurt.

The road to these depths looks so inviting and the incline is actually so gradual that it doesn't appear steep at all. If it looked steep, we would see the trap, and most of us would just turn away. The road doesn't seem difficult until we are so far in that when we want to get off this road, but we realize we can't climb out of the ditch. Our feet begin to lose traction and we start the slippery decline. Pretty soon we feel like we are on a waterslide picking up speed as our momentum carries us downward. Way too late we realize that our "valuable earthly treasures" are adding to the momentum.

I think that's what happened to our sister Eve. One minute she was strolling through the wildflowers minding her own business, and the next minute something shiny (in her case, forbidden fruit) caught her eye. The ever looming "snake in the grass" was right there all too willing to help her reach for that fruit. I'm a woman, and I know how quickly that glimmer of a shiny object can catch our eye. The shiny object that leads to destruction can be material, physical, and even emotional. Anything that draws us away from the living room and into the kitchen, away from our Father, can be harmful.

One of my "shiny objects" is sugar. I can be completely oblivious to an elephant standing next to me, but I can smell chocolate in the next county. While sugary treats aren't completely evil, the over-indulgence of them can lead to a full-blown addiction that can actually catapult us into the depths. For me, sugar is a migraine trigger. It's an addiction that will send me spiraling very quickly, and it does not end well! As I shared earlier, I have also found out that sugar isn't just a trigger for migraines; it is also toxic to my body! Satan and his cronies have studied us enough to know our every weakness, and they are hell-bent on providing every tempting situation possible to trick us into giving in to our weaknesses. Satan makes it his business to take us out, and he considers his mission very seriously. In fact, it's a life and death matter to him–ours!

Several years ago, my husband and I were helping our kids move into a townhouse together. Directly inside the front door was a very large, built-in TV cabinet with a very large TV in it. The TV was on with the volume quite loud. I'm sure I must have walked past that very loud TV at least a dozen or more times. I again walked past the TV up the stairs to my son's room and asked quite seriously, "Do you guys have a TV?" I know, right? It's amazing that these children have survived to adulthood. It's purely by the grace of God (and a really good dad). So before anyone had a chance to close their gaping mouths and shake their heads in disbelief, I spied a box of Oatmeal Cream Pies under my son's night stand, on the floor, completely out of sight (to anyone except a sugar addict) and said, "Can I have one of your oatmeal cookies?" Again, they all stood there in total disbelief. Can you blame them? I saw what I wanted to see, and what I wanted to see was exactly what "fed," literally, a weakness – a fairly innocent one, or so I thought.

The point is this: let's think twice about judging Martha, or anyone else for that matter. I know my slope is slippery, and if I don't keep my eyes and ears tuned to Jesus (and I mean tuned in, like a mosquito to bare skin), I will start slipping and sliding all over the place. But the good news is that God wins! You know why satan is so mad at Him? Because He won! He won before this cosmic battle began, He wins now, and He wins in the end. It makes me crazy in love with Him. It's the biggest party this side of heaven. Our sins are forgiven. No pit is ever too deep or slimy or dark or ugly for His hands to reach down and pluck us right out. Just three words from our desperate lips are all it takes: "Jesus help me." Who could have imagined that God has arms so long to reach so far? I kind of get this silly vision of Gumby with arms stretching and stretching and stretching. He reaches those long arms right down, plucks us up, washes off the mud, cleanses our wounds and loves us like we are some kind of awesome. "I waited patiently for the Lord; He turned to me and heard my cry. He lifted me out of the slimy pit, out of the mud and mire; he set my feet on a rock and gave me a firm place to stand," Psalm 40:1-2.

What does this have to do with Martha? I'm only speculating, but I'm willing to bet that at some point she too pulled up the tent stakes of her heart and moved to a better neighborhood. Let's give her the benefit of the doubt. Let's trust that she learned some valuable things from her faux pas that so unfortunately got hung out there like dirty laundry for the whole world to see. I'm sorry for her, really I am, but I'm so thankful it's her and not me in the annals of history. My depths are so deep and depraved that Martha and I aren't even in the same universe.

I know some of you may think that your depths are too deep and you've gone too far this time even for God. Well there's a snake in the grass that's lying to you, and he'll stop at nothing to prevent you from moving on. He'll fluff your pillow and put a chocolate or two on it to keep you happy there. Let me implore you to lift your eyes and heart to Jesus, who is ready to rescue you at a moment's notice. "The Lord upholds ALL those who fall and lifts ALL who are bowed down," Psalm 145:14 (emphasis added).

5

Warrior Heart

I ask God a lot of questions. In fact, I constantly barrage Him with an endless stream of inquiries. If I come to Him as a little child, then I am like the three-year-old that never stops asking "why" and "what" and "when" and "how!" I have this insatiable curiosity that would get me in trouble were it not for my Daddy reining me in, slowing me down, and catching my feet before they again head for those slippery slopes. Tonight, as I write in the quiet darkness of my home, I am asking Him to lift the veil and let my eyes see the Spirit realm with clarity. My heart longs to see both the heavenly activity and the demonic activity with wisdom and accuracy.

I'm not looking for trouble, but I'm a warrior at heart. Warriors can smell a good fight. Long ago, I learned this truth, "For our struggle is not against flesh and blood, but against the rulers, against the powers of this dark world and against the spiritual forces of evil in the heavenly realms," Eph. 6:12. I ask the Lord to show me the plans of the enemy so I can walk in victory at all times. Of course, we must be clothed with wisdom, discernment, and humility at all times, and NEVER be caught without our armor. Our armor is depicted in Scripture as the belt of truth, the breastplate of righteousness, the shoes of peace, the shield of faith, the helmet of salvation, and the sword of the Spirit (Eph. 6:13-17). We need this armor to fight against satan – they are the only weapons that protect us against his evil schemes.

The enemy has stolen so much from me. While I was still in my mother's womb, he put a target on my back and aimed his slimy arrows smack dab at its center. As I said earlier,

Can I Just be Real?

I was born with life-threatening asthma, spent most of my life in and out of hospitals, have had enough surgeries that I should have had a zipper installed, experienced paralyzing depression and anxiety, and have taken a long walk on the wild side of life.

After my traumatizing experience with babysitters, I was eventually old enough to stay home by myself. As I said, we lived in the country and I was isolated. My only friends were my many cats and the family dog. A very traumatic event for me was losing that faithful companion. My parents took me on a weeklong vacation and left the dog home alone. Needless to say, he was gone when we got home. My suspicions were never confirmed, but many times the neighbor had threatened to shoot him. He was my best friend in a world surrounded by loneliness. The lesson I came away with was, "Don't trust and don't let anyone get close. It will hurt!"

As a teenager, the pain began to surface as anger and resentment. The walls around my heart were firmly established. Most nights I would cry myself to sleep. I would listen to my parents argue about whose turn it was to "talk to me." Neither of them wanted to deal with this emotional child night after night. It wasn't that they didn't love me. They just didn't know what to do with me.

By the time I was in high school my mistrust and loneliness was in full swing. My parents didn't allow me to attend school activities, so my social life was quite non-existent. They did not know the Lord, so I didn't either. I felt socially awkward and aimless. For my graduation gift they gave me a set of luggage and told me they had made the decision to enroll me in a community college sixty miles away. I felt like a scared bird being kicked out of my nest. It was a dysfunctional nest, but a nest, nonetheless.

Satan had been watching. I was a lost sheep with no Shepherd. I was easy prey! I was looking for somewhere to belong and someone to care. The enemy moved in for the kill. The wrong people appeared at the right time and my baggage began to pile up fast and furious. College was a fast lane of alcohol, parties, men without an ounce of integrity, bars, marijuana, and anything that would dull my senses. I might have cried out to Jesus, but I didn't know who He was, and satan was happy to keep it that way.

I didn't meet my heavenly Father until I was thirty years old, which I will share more about later. Because I didn't know him yet, I took a lot of hits while navigating those slippery slopes that I chose to explore. In hindsight, I know He had my back, I just didn't know at the time that He was there. The very same "snake" that cornered Eve in the Garden had my name and address memorized. He knew exactly which buttons to push and when. My actions seemed so fun to me at the time, but the road of those early years was littered with baggage and trash, lies and deception, and little direction. Satan used every trick to keep me in bondage and away from the One who would set me free.

In Biblical times when a king was conquered he would be publically humiliated. The victorious king would make him lie on the ground while putting his foot on the neck of the defeated, humiliated captive to show his victory! Sound familiar? It sure does to me. Jesus put His foot on satan's neck the day He spoke those three beautiful words from the cross, "It is finished." It's over! I'm not in bondage to satan anymore, and that target on my back is covered by two beautiful nail-pierced hands. I may have some scars, but those scars fuel my burning passion to push past all obstacles straight for the place where the heart of my Father dwells. I want nothing but Him. I have been forgiven, redeemed, and pulled from the pit. I will still lace up my army boots and fight when I need to, but my battles are now fought from a completely different place. I no longer try to contend in my own strength or my own wisdom. The trials have made me stronger and more dependent on Jesus than I ever would have been without them. When we begin to see battles as our heavenly Father sees them, although not perfected yet, our eyes and ears are more fine-tuned to His heart, and we realize He knows far better when to fight and when to be silent. It is from a place of humility and total abandon to Him that we gain our strength. We are so hidden in Him that we no longer need to fear even the worst the enemy has to throw at us. We fight from a place of love and peace. What the enemy stole from me has developed in me a warrior heart.

Last year was a year of soul searching and healing for me, which involved going through my own "fiery furnace." I'm not talking about hot flashes, although they do rear their ugly head from time to time. I was led to revisit my past and unload some of that baggage that I'd been hanging on to for way too long. Wounds that are inflicted when we are innocent and naïve can create scars that can harden in our souls. These wounds can lie dormant for years, or even decades, but they will eventually surface. They form who we are and how we process life, without us really even knowing it. Sometimes they become infected and throb with pain, and sometimes they seep and bleed a little or a lot and we just don't know what to do with them. We usually put a bandage on and hope it won't fall off to reveal the ugly mess that it is.

Let's get real – none of us really want to drag that baggage out of the closet! After all these years, it is moldy and smelly and it stings our eyes as we peer into it. Sometimes there are skeletons that we would prefer to keep there. Sometimes there are gaping wounds and blood and guts still too raw. Sometimes there are bruises and scars that continue to remind us of the pain that was first inflicted. We all have them! No one is exempt. Some are more painful than others, and they come with carry-on bags full of unforgiveness, bitterness, envy, jealousy, tears, and heartbreak.

This year, the Lord decided it was time for me to get those suitcases out and start unloading. I have had two colonoscopies and a root canal that paled in comparison to this!

I had to go back to when I was about five or six years old as that very sad, lonely little girl, and one by one, begin to unpack the pain and the scars. However, there was one significant difference this time. I now was looking at that little girl through the eyes of a Daddy who cried when she cried, hurt when she hurt, and never left her side – not for one single moment. I saw it all through His tender eyes filled with compassion and love. It was probably one of the most painful things I have ever experienced, but it was more necessary than even drawing my next breath. It had to come out; and then it had to go. It had been in that closet way too long and it was beginning to rot and stink!

Some of my dearest friends and my husband lovingly sat weeping with me as I went back (in my heart) all those decades to that little girl and said goodbye to her. She was unkempt, scruffy, sad, and confused as she stood in the yard of her childhood home, bearing the scars of innocence lost. I watched (in my spirit) as Jesus bent down and picked her up in His arms, hugged her, wiped away her tears, and held her close. I needed to see her one more time and know that she was safe with Jesus now, and it was finally ok to let go. I tearfully said good bye as I squared my shoulders and walked away, not as a wounded little child, but as a daughter of the King who was now healed, redeemed, and whole. I had opened the closet, took out the hurts one by one, picked off the scabs, let them bleed, and then gave them to my Daddy to let his healing balm do its work.

I won't lie. It hurt – really bad. It's so much easier to hide our scars than to pick off the scabs and let them bleed all over. It's easier to try to ignore the skeletons and the moldy suitcases and the carry-ons with their plethora of ugliness than it is to face them and admit we are harboring bitterness, unforgiveness and fear. I have had to face not only wounds caused by others, but wounds caused by my own stupidity and sinful nature. It was like dirty laundry that had been in the basket WAY too long and should have spent a good week soaking, but out it came, piece by dirty piece.

And guess what? Just like that colonoscopy I mentioned earlier, it wasn't much fun, but when it was all over I sure felt good – clean, light and free. If we want a warrior heart and if we want to develop a real authenticity with Jesus, ourselves, and others, we have to let the Lord heal our past, or the enemy will fling those suitcases wide open and take advantage of every piece of that soiled past. If we hold on to even a hint of anger, unforgiveness, bitterness, or woundedness, he won't hesitate for a split second to use it against us. It's a dangerous business, and we must be nestled safely in the arms of our Father at all times. We must be poised and ready for that roaring lion, and the only way to accomplish this is to be free of the baggage that is dragging us down. Retreat is not an option! We must face our enemies head on, even if those enemies are sometimes ourselves.

If you haven't scoured your closets yet, I suggest you gather your closest friends around you, ask the Lord to show you how to move forward, and dare to open a suitcase. It may hurt for a bit, but the pain will be but a distant memory in comparison to the freedom. Cry when you need to, repent, forgive, and let your Daddy's love wash over you. Take breaks when you must, go slowly, be methodical, ask the Lord to reveal places you need to go, and be brave! You can do this. You have my permission to eat as much chocolate as you need. You have a warrior's heart. Keep well-grounded by seeking Jesus above all else. Allow yourself time to heal.

❧ 6 ◈
What did You Say?

I love hearing my Daddy talk to me. He can say anything, even if it's a reprimand; I just love the sound of His voice. Have you ever loved someone so much that the sound of their voice made you stop dead in your tracks and perk up your ears? That's how I feel when my heavenly Daddy speaks to me. Sometimes it's a whisper. Sometimes it's a shout! Sometimes it's a song or a bird chirping. Sometimes it's scripture, or just a "knowing" in my Spirit. But I'm a work in progress, and I wonder how many times I'm just too preoccupied to hear Him!

Do you complain that God is silent and then realize that your radio is blasting, the T.V. is blaring, the baby is crying, your nose is in a magazine, and the only time your mouth is silent is when it is filled with food? There's a reason silence is called golden – it's expensive! Silence can be painful. We're all familiar with the childhood "Quiet Game" where a silence-seeking parent coerces their children into a game that requires no talking in order to win. Confession: I was worse at it than my kids. The silence was so hard for me to handle, that I would cheat! "Did the doorbell just ring?" "Who fed the dog beans?" and "What time is it?" Those that know me well know that if I'm quiet for longer than two minutes, I'll fall asleep. I have been known to fall asleep standing up, lying on a concrete floor, petting the cat, taking a bath, pretending to listen to someone, or any moment that involves a two second pause! My point is, sometimes I'm so busy filling the silence with questions, that I miss the voice of the Lord answering them.

Thankfully, our Father knows us and has the patience of, well…God! He can find a million ways to tell us the same thing over and over until we get it right, and then he cheers for us like we're some kind of geniuses. It's truly a parent's love. For example, every time our kids used the potty chair we acted like they just won the Olympics. You know – cheers, M & M's and high fives. He loves us the same way!

I love the way God loves: unconditionally, purely, and in spite of our every shortcoming and flaw. Sometimes I look in the mirror and tell the Holy Spirit that I'm so sorry that He has to live in my body. Think about it for a minute – morning breath, sweat, wrinkles, all those extra fat cells, sags and bags, and everything else that comes with humanity. Add to that the propensity to go my own way, my ability to overlook victories and focus on failures, and the general challenges of a heart that is constantly being renewed. But He forgives, He loves through it all, and His mercies are new every morning. I am pretty grateful for His tenacity and for His heart that never gives up on me. This is not a job for the faint of heart. Who could love us more than He does?

One of my favorite characteristics of God is His sense of humor. Do you know that God is really, really fun? He has the best sense of humor; it's just a part of who He is. "He will fill your mouth with laughter," Job 8:21. Just look at nature. It is full of crazy creatures. There are birds, sea creatures, monkeys, and all sorts of unimaginable silly-looking things! I can laugh until I cry watching kittens play and frolic. I love to laugh. Sadly, I don't laugh near enough anymore; but a good laugh, especially from my Daddy, will bless me more than anything else this world could possibly offer me. It truly is medicine for the soul.

I didn't always appreciate laughter as much as I do now. As a young wife and mother I was often overwhelmed. I had friends who would gather together with our children, but I rarely got out by myself. I was often crabby at my kids and husband. One of these friends invited me to a Christian women's event which met once a month. She explained it to me this way, "You get to drop your kids off at a local church for free babysitting, go to a restaurant and pay only three dollars for a small brunch. You have to listen to a speaker talk about something spiritual for an hour, and then you visit with other ladies before picking up your kids." It sounded good to me! So, once a month for a year, I went to my grown-up outing. At the end of each meeting the speaker would pray and give an invitation to receive Jesus as Lord and Savior of our lives. I would politely bow my head and think about what I was going to feed my kids for lunch.

The month before my thirtieth birthday I truly believe the Lord decided to take matters into His own hands. I had avoided Him long enough, and it was time to get serious. As the speaker asked us to bow our heads for prayer, I politely bowed as usual and let my mind wander. But, this time was different. I honestly do not remember making a decision or commitment but I felt a peace come over me that was not of this world. I looked up dazed and confused not knowing what to do next. I went home knowing something was different, but I didn't know what. The peace stayed with me and I began to change inside. I stopped screaming at my kids, and became more calm and patient. The next month I pulled aside one of the women who had been nice to me there and told her what happened. She smiled her beautiful smile and told me I had let Jesus come into my heart. She began to mentor me and led me to a wonderful church family. To this day she is my sister-in-Christ, sent by God as a blessing to walk beside me. We have been through some very turbulent times as well as very sweet times together. She is one of the few people I have given access to my guarded heart.

I would lay awake almost every night talking to my new friend Jesus, and asking to know everything about Him. I was never tired the next day. I had supernatural energy and grace. I wanted to know everything I had missed over the years, and would spend hours questioning and listening. For a while, it was beautiful. We just talked and hung out and laughed as He shared His heart with me. Having not grown up knowing the Lord or being part of the body of Christ, I had no biblical preconceived ideas or teachings. I came to Him innocently and naïvely in that amazing experience. I spent every spare minute of the day reading, listening, laughing, and crying as I soaked in His presence.

But something very sad happened to me that set me back to a low place on my journey. As I began getting connected with other brothers and sisters, my excitement flowed over like Niagara Falls. In my newfound joy, I told everyone about my conversations with Jesus. From the Christian community, I began hearing words that started me on a trail of doubt – things like, "God doesn't talk to us like that," "Those stories in the Bible are only parables," "You will mature and the excitement will wear off," "God doesn't really move mountains," "The Holy Spirit doesn't move today," and on and on. Sadly, I began to believe the lies; remember the snake in the grass? He's still alive and well. My excitement began to fade and I began to doubt. I began to think things like, "Maybe that wasn't God talking to me; maybe it was my imagination." "Don't talk about it, worship quietly; don't draw attention to yourself, slow down."

Such lies! Don't EVER let anyone put you or God in a box! EVER! You WILL make mistakes and you WILL fall. We are human and will get messy, but our Father is bigger than any mess we could ever make. Almost daily I pray for three things – wisdom, humility, and discernment. If we can be humble and repent, then we can trust that our Daddy has it covered.

"This then is how we know that we belong to the truth and how we set our hearts at rest in His presence whenever our hearts condemn us; for God is greater than our hearts and He knows everything. Dear friends if our hearts do not condemn us, we have confidence before God and receive from Him," 1 John 3:19-22.

He knows our hearts! If your heart has a hunger for your Father, then get out of that box and worship with abandon! You talk to Him and with Him! Don't sneak around; shout Him from the rooftops! Put your feet on the floor every morning and make satan tremble! Don't ever let anyone quench that beautiful Spirit living in you!

After years of doubt had stolen my confidence, my Daddy began to put a hunger for Him back into my heart. I refused to settle and be quiet any longer. There was more and I wanted it. I didn't know how I knew there was more, but I began to hunger like a starving lion. I got mad! I growled! I attacked people I shouldn't have and I spoke when I should have been quiet. But I couldn't help it! Again that snake stole from me, but this time he barked up the wrong tree. Never mess with a hungry lioness! I declared freedom for myself and, an all-out war on the enemy of my soul. This time I spent years begging my Daddy to teach me and train me to never be deceived in this way again. I wanted to be sold out, and I wanted that crazy-lady passion back.

In my passion, I was totally ignorant of the cost of telling God that I would do anything or go anywhere, and I dove right into the spiritual river, completely over my head! My hunger for Him fueled my chasing Him, until He caught me. The cry of my soul was to hear His voice clearly again, but my confidence was shaken from others speaking doubt into me. Paralyzed by the thought of making those same mistakes, I was having a hard time moving forward.

One afternoon, I was playing hangman on my computer, and I heard, "Do you want to practice hearing Me?" Slightly stunned, and a little surprised, I answered, "Yes!" As I listened, I began to hear letters in my mind, and as I heard them, I typed them out on the hangman game. The word spelled out exactly perfect with no mistakes. No man hanging! I did it again, and again, and again! Then I heard nothing, and I lost the game. Hanged! I promise this is true! A couple weeks later I was playing Bible Trivia with my kids, and I started hearing answers. If you know this game, some of the questions are totally obscure, and I was batting a thousand! The kids accused me of cheating. I was laughing so hard I almost fell off the chair! This was way too much fun. Of course I was cheating! How do you tell your kids that God is giving you the answers to Bible Trivia? They already thought I was crazy and this would only confirm it!

In the next weeks, my hearing became more and more tuned in to the Lord's voice: my son went out with friends – I knew where he was and what he was doing. My daughter went out, and I knew where she was and exactly what time she would walk in the door. I knew things, I won games, and it made my family crazy!

Here's the thing, He had to build my confidence again. I needed to know when it was His voice and when it was not. I'm way too ignorant and impulsive to be trusted on my own. I'm still learning! I still mess up and don't always hear perfectly. At times, my impulsive nature sends me sprawling out flat on my face (but what a great place to get humble fast). Life is a journey, not a destination, and we are constantly being formed into His likeness as we tune our ears to His voice.

So many people say, "I don't hear God." Friends, you may not hear Him today or tomorrow but you WILL hear Him. He wants you to hear Him; go read your Bible. No one ever lost a battle when they consulted God first. He made sure they heard Him loud and clear. Sometimes people asked for a ridiculous amount of confirmations. If they truly asked from a pure heart, He never turned them down.

If you truly want to hear your Father's voice, then ask, and don't take no for an answer. If someone pursued me relentlessly just because they wanted to hear me talk to them

What did You Say?

do you think I would ignore them? Would I turn them away? Maybe, if they were crazy, but God doesn't work that way. He takes the crazy people right where they are and turns them into amazing crazy warriors! Be aware that we all hear God speak differently. He is infinitely creative and He knows what will resonate with each unique individual. Don't try to copy someone else or feel inadequate because you hear Him differently.

Friends, persistence pays off. I have a reputation for being determined, my husband knows this well, so do my friends, so does God. I'm pretty sure His door has a well-worn groove in it from me knocking. If He doesn't answer, I keep knocking. I'm stubborn that way. You should be too! He WILL answer. Maybe not exactly when you want, but He will answer. Sometimes you won't like His answer, but you asked, and now you have to accept it. Remember, His ways are not our ways and we won't always understand. I have come to trust that He knows the beginning and the end and everything in between and it will go well for me if I let Him have the steering wheel. Driving's not my strong suit anyway!

So put on your goggles and dive right in. The water will be cold at first and a bit murky, but before you know it, you'll be swimming like a pro. The current will be rapid in places and still in others and sometimes you will have to paddle like crazy just to stay afloat. But there will be those sweet seasons where you can just float downstream soaking up the sunshine without a care in the world. Oh sweet thing, I will be right there beside you paddling and floating. It's a great journey! Let's all hold hands and wade in until we are way over our heads in His glory.

7
Crisis of Faith

Have you ever snorted when you laughed? If you answered yes to this, you are my new best friend. I have a dear friend who is one of the few people who will watch Mr. Bean movies with me. Every time we watch them I laugh so hard I snort. She loves me so much that she will endure the movie just so she can laugh at me snorting. It's truly an act of love because she is not impressed by Mr. Bean. I think he is hilarious, but I also am very easily entertained. I will laugh at myself so hard I snort and will be the only one in the room "in on the joke." As Emerson Eggerich says in *Love and Respect*, "not wrong, just different."[1] For some reason "different" is a word people seem to use a lot to describe me. I probably should be offended, but I prefer to believe they are laughing "with" me and not "at" me.

Do you think Martha snorted? She was probably snorting just a little as she put up with Mary and her propensity to neglect her kitchen duties, but I'm pretty sure it wasn't accompanied by laughter. Laughter is good. I wish Martha would have laughed more and worried less. I wish I would laugh more and worry less! If you have children you know what I mean about worry. I used to worry about them when they were sick. I worried about them when I left them with a babysitter. I worried about them when they went to nursery school. I really worried about them when they started high school. But thankfully, a wise friend told me that we have a Father who doesn't want us to worry or be anxious about anything. This wise friend told me to visualize walking my children up a flight of stairs where Jesus is standing at the top, putting them in his arms, and walking back down the stairs, leaving them there in His arms. I will be honest – it took me many, many tries, but eventually I was able to visualize taking them up the steps, putting them in His lap, turning around, and walking away. Done! They were safely in the arms of Jesus, and there was no more reason to worry. It actually worked quite well. I seldom worried about them even after they began to drive or went away to college or even now, as they have children of their own. Now I have grandchildren to safely tuck away on Jesus' lap.

What a blessing to worry less and laugh more. I can relax and truly enjoy the journey now. I still worry at times, but have learned that as soon as I give it back to my Daddy, I can relax and trust Him with those I love so much. It doesn't mean that there will never be trials or pain; it just means that I can trust Him with whatever comes. Whew! Martha, all I can say is calm down, kick back the recliner, and put dinner in the slow cooker next time.

Many years ago when my son was in high school, he was involved in a very serious car accident. It was the last day of his junior year, and after school he came home and asked if he could drive to a neighboring town to do some shopping. Against our better judgment, we let him go and take my car, which was a small, Chevy Nova. For about a month the Lord had been talking to me about trust, challenging me to trust Him with everything. Every magazine article I read was about trust, everything I heard spoken was about trust, and every scripture I read was about trust. Many times He would ask me, "Do you trust Me?" I had no idea what was about to come, but I prayed to be able to trust Him enough to pass whatever test was ahead.

About two hours after my son left, I was in the kitchen making supper and heard these words in my mind: "Your son has been in an accident." Before I even had a chance to register the words, the phone rang, and someone asked to speak to my husband. As my husband listened to the person on the line, the look on his face told me what I knew I didn't want to hear: our son had been in an accident and was on his way to the hospital. As we ran to our car, I said to the Lord, "He is Yours. Whatever happens, whether You take him or allow us to have him longer, I give him to You. I trust You!" I heard the still small voice of the Lord gently speak to me that our son was going to be fine, so I felt peace as we made the trip to join him at the hospital. Because the Lord had assured me that he was fine, I fully expected to arrive and see him sitting up with maybe a broken arm and a few bruises. I was not prepared for what we saw. As we pulled into the parking lot, he was being loaded into a helicopter. He was unconscious and bloody. We were told he had head and chest trauma, a collapsed lung, a broken jaw, several broken bones, and was in serious condition. The EMT calmly told us that they were taking him to a larger hospital eighty miles away and they would arrive in twenty minutes. He asked us to drive carefully and not to speed.

Have you ever been faced with a decision whether to believe what your eyes see and your ears hear, or to believe what the Lord tells you? Many times He has spoken to me about "living in my Spirit" versus "living in the world," but until that moment I hadn't ever really put it into practice. "Do I believe what the Lord is telling me or do I believe what the world is saying?" I came face to face with a life-changing decision, and I had to decide which path I was going to travel.

The ninety-minute trip to the hospital was quiet. I had some serious conversations with the Lord as I pointed out that our son didn't "look" okay, and his injuries seemed serious. How could the Lord tell me he was fine, when it was plain to see these were not just a few bruises? The unknown looked pretty scary at this moment. What did I believe? I was having a crisis of faith. All I could do was ask the Lord to give my shaking body His peace and to quiet my raging mind. My heart believed and trusted the Lord, but my body

Can I Just be Real?

and mind were reacting to the trauma. Several times I repeated to my husband that our son was fine and that he wouldn't be taken from us. I didn't have the clarity of mind to share with Him that this reassurance was from the Lord, so he thought I was just trying to convince myself. At some point the peace that truly passes all understanding settled into my very soul, and a calm that I still struggle to describe came over me.

At first, my husband thought my calm was denial. As the days wore on with our precious child in ICU, my calm began to wear on his nerves. We didn't talk about it; we just coped as best we could. It wasn't until much later that I told my husband the full story of my conversations with the Lord and how He had promised our son would have a full recovery. I was still trying to process as best I could and understand what was happening. I wish I could say that I believed without question and my faith was unshakeable, but my Daddy and I had many long conversations over the next several days as we worked through this. After our son spent many days in ICU and more time in a regular room, we went home with our precious cargo, pain meds, no solid food, an ended football career, a long summer of recovery ahead, and thankful hearts.

Looking back, I am in awe. This is not something I would wish on any mother. It was the worst phone call I have ever received, and I never want another one like it. EVER! When the Lord tells you that your child is fine and then you see circumstances that completely conflict with His word to you, you have some choices to make. They will test you to the core. Is it really the Lord speaking to me or is it my wishful thinking? How do I process what my eyes see and my ears hear against what the Holy Spirit is telling me? My eyes aren't lying to me; I know what I see. How could my heart make a split second choice to give my only son back to his heavenly Father, if that was what He was asking of me? How could I have a peace that was humanly indescribable?

In my Daddy's grace He prepared me long before I had to make this choice. He spoke to me gently and tenderly about trust and letting go, and taught me a life lesson that I will take with me until my last breath on this earth: trust not what my eyes see, trust what my spirit hears, listen with my heart and soul and Holy Spirit within me. We do not belong to this world; we are only passing through. We are not bound to the economy of this earth; we are woven into the fabric of a heavenly tapestry where things are not always as they seem. So, let's try to enjoy the journey. Our Father has us covered. It won't always be easy, and it won't always have a storybook ending. Sometimes, we will send loved ones on ahead of us; sometimes, we will keep them for a while longer. Either way, we can trust our Father to give us the peace we will need for the road ahead. Pain will come, but so will joy. Sometimes we have to mix those salty tears with our snorts of laughter, but we will cry and laugh together. I'm sure glad I don't have to travel these winding roads alone. My sweet friend, your Heavenly Father saves every tear you shed. "You keep track of all my sorrows. You have collected all my tears in your bottle. You have recorded each one in your book," Psalm 56:8 NLT.

He always has His arms wrapped tightly around you. There will come a day when we will never shed another tear as we spend eternity with loved ones and live our forever with unspeakable joy.

8

Fire Walkers

It's a snowy Wednesday afternoon, and there are seven women engaged in worship in my home. One is face down on the floor, one is on her knees, and a few are standing in the dining room swaying to the music with hands raised to heaven. One is on her knees in the kitchen gently sobbing, and one is looking out the window, gazing at the snow covered trees. I step over bodies and dodge outstretched arms as I mix in my own worship while I stir the pot of soup simmering on the stove.

We all have one thing in common: with one heart we cry to the Lord for nothing more than His face. We approach His throne as unadorned, imperfect daughters who desire to know more of Him. Worship lingers longer than usual as we feel the gentle presence of our Daddy begin to fill the atmosphere. No one is in a hurry. No one is concerned with how they look. Bodies are strewn around the house with eyes closed. Gentle weeping and quiet cries for more of Him penetrate the stillness. Worship rises like smoke from incense. Our hearts are laid bare, surrendered to our Heavenly Father. As I listen from the kitchen, I hear prayers emerging quietly from hearts pierced by Him, but not the usual list of wants and needs and must haves, not the Santa Claus, slot-machine kind of wish list. Instead, hearts begin to ask Him what He wants. What is our Father's heart? What does He desire?

Collectively, we ask ourselves: what if we were to bless Him instead of always asking Him to bless us? What does that look like? What if we were to quietly listen to His heart and then lift that heart back to Him as daughters sold out for only one thing: to dwell in the house of the Lord forever.

"One thing I ask of the Lord – this is what I seek: that I may dwell in the house of the Lord all the days of my life," Psalm 27:4.

This is what was happening that ordinary Wednesday afternoon when a group of women dared to put down their usual busyness and be still before their Daddy. We didn't expect it to happen this way. All we knew is that we were tired of seeking the presents and were hungry for the Presence. We were finding joy in blessing the Lord in the inner courts of praise, and we never wanted to leave.

Let me explain briefly the inner and outer courts. The Jewish Temple was divided into courts and rooms based on their function. There was an outer court which was available for anyone to enter. Animals were sold for sacrifice. Money changed hands, and the sick and poor lingered in hopes of being noticed. As you can imagine, it was chaotic, noisy and dirty. This is also where Jesus drove out the money changers and rebuked them. The outer court is where people came to socialize and prepare their sacrifices. They bought and ate food and often jockeyed for prominence. The ministering that went on in the outer court was to people. Amidst the chaos and noise of animals, filth, and a plethora of people of every social status, there were no restrictions. Anyone was allowed to enter the outer court at any time and without any required cleansing.

In contrast, the inner court was reserved for only the priests. It was a very holy place where priests alone were allowed to minister to the Lord. They were only allowed to enter at specific times and were required to observe a very strict cleansing process before entering with holy awe. It was there in this holy inner court where the heart of the Lord could be truly found.

The outer court no longer holds appeal to me with its clanging and clamoring for more. People are always looking but never finding enough to fill their bellies, their wallets or their closets with the next best thing that comes along. The sights and sounds of the world drown out the quiet whispers of my Daddy. Few ever get past this outer court. Not because we can't, but because we have lost all vision, passion, and zeal to dare travel past the chaos we have come to accept as normal. It's comfortable out there. It's lonely in the inner court. The quiet can be deafening. Our ears and eyes need time to adjust to the stillness where the heart of our Daddy dwells.

Access to this holy place is available to us now because the veil separating the inner and outer courts was torn when Jesus died on the cross. "At that moment the curtain of the temple was torn in two from top to bottom. The earth shook and the rocks split," Matt. 27:51. This sacrifice of God's only Son was to provide access to God's heart without going through the priests. We now have access to His holy court, but we must take it seriously and remember we are entering the Holy of Holies. We must be willing to be purified and cleansed as we transition from the noisy outer court of focusing on others or ourselves, to the inner court of ministering to the Lord Himself.

There is something that stands between us and that sweet inner court. Something that few want to encounter and even fewer are willing to endure to the end: the Refiner's Fire. It's an all-consuming furnace that burns hotter than any of us could imagine. The flames lick away at our flesh, demons come screaming out, and closet doors are flung wide open. It's a lonely place – just you and God – opening old baggage, evicting skeletons, shining the spotlight on pride and jealousy. In the fire, our flesh, the old nature that is so opposed to God, is stripped away while He works to prepare us for the journey from the outer to inner court. The inner court is much too pure to allow the flesh to enter. It must all be burned away, leaving only a cleansed and purified heart.

Why must we go through this fire? Why would a good Father allow us to suffer and endure pain? Let's take a look at some of the "firewalkers" in the Bible and see if they can shed any light on this question.

Daniel had life pretty good until he and his friends ended up being torn from their homes and dragged off to a foreign land to become slaves. It was through no fault of their own, but they were the victims of a nation who turned its back on God. Daniel did everything right yet ended up in the fire of adversity (Daniel 6). I believe God knew He could trust Daniel to stand firm and true even when his life was on the line. Remember the lion's den? Daniel would not compromise his faith in his God even if it meant facing down some hungry lions. Whether he lived or died he would not deny his God. In the end, God delivered him; but even if He hadn't, Daniel would not compromise. The purpose? King Darius, the very one who had Daniel thrown in the lion's den, was led to proclaim "The Living God who endures forever, His kingdom will not be destroyed, and His dominion will never end. He rescues and He saves for He rescued Daniel from the lion's den," Daniel 6:26-27. The king then issued a decree that in every part of his kingdom all people must fear and reverence the God of Daniel. Daniel endured this trial so that God would be exalted. Hardened hearts turned to God because Daniel dared to stand apart.

Let's not forget Daniel's friends Shadrach, Meshach and Abednego who were thrown into a literal furnace because they would rather give up their lives than worship anyone other than the One, the true God. (Daniel 3). Again, God rescued them from the furnace and they came out not even smelling of smoke. Why? In a land filled with idol worship and wickedness, godly people were willing to stand apart, go through the "fiery furnace," and turn an evil nation into one who worshiped the true Holy God.

In both cases, all it took was someone who was willing to go through a fire, even risking their own lives, for an entire nation to be redeemed. This is what an intimate relationship of trust and faith with our Father can do.

Joseph's situation was different, but the fire in his life still accomplished great things (Genesis 37). Joseph was a golden child, one who could do no wrong in his father's eyes. Sounds like the beginning of a perfect storm doesn't it? Joseph saw no signs of a furnace looming in his future as he enjoyed the good life as a spoiled, favorite son. However, the Lord gave Joseph a dream of a bright future that he just couldn't help sharing with his less-than-enthusiastic brothers. They didn't like him to begin with, and this display of pride did not help. They plotted to kill him, but God had other plans. They ended up selling Joseph into slavery, and he was hauled off to a foreign land in chains. I'm sure by then Joseph wondered what just happened and where his bright future that the Lord had promised him had gone. Sound familiar?

When things don't go the way we planned or life takes a sudden turn for the worse, we immediately fall apart and accuse God of selling us down the road. We don't see the big picture and the need for a little refining along the way. If Joseph would have been sent to Egypt and immediately been exalted to a position of leadership in Pharaoh's palace, he would have still been an arrogant, spoiled child, who would have been ill-prepared for the destiny God had for him. An entire nation was at stake; Joseph would be the one to bring the Israelite nation to Egypt. Joseph endured some tough times along his journey, including prison, but God was with him as He is also with us. Joseph matured from a spoiled child into a man of integrity and humility. How? By submitting to God's refining hand and allowing the Lord to prune and refine him when necessary. It wasn't easy and didn't happen overnight, but he grew into a man God could use in mighty ways. He discovered an intimacy with the Lord that he never would have had if he hadn't been forced out of his privileged comfort zone. The trials Joseph endured made him into a man God could trust. Not only was Egypt saved from famine, but Joseph's entire family was also saved from certain death in the famine. Because of the Lord's favor, Joseph prospered and Israel grew into a great nation. Joseph made peace with his brothers and was reunited with his father.

Dear one, when life doesn't go our way and when things seem to go in the opposite direction of what we thought we heard God tell us, it's not because He has abandoned us. When we have hopes and dreams that seem to tarry or be derailed, we must press forward and let God do his pruning and refining. We may not all be called to redeem a nation, but we all have a destiny that only we can fulfill. I know the fire hurts. None of us want to see the lions' den looming or feel the heat of the furnace; but we are in good company. The pages of scripture are filled from front to back with those who experienced pride turned to humility, arrogance tempered, selfishness transformed to love, hearts of stone softened into hearts of compassion, and as a result received the sweet intimacy that only comes from testing and stretching. Don't give up when the road gets hard and the journey seems long; God's refining you to be the gold that you were created to be.

I recently had a dream in which the Lord showed me a room-sized furnace with a large door on the front. The fire was red hot, and bars of gold had been placed on grates inside. As the gold began to melt, it formed into small nuggets that fell through the grates onto the floor of the furnace. Many people were waiting in line for a turn to put on a fireproof suit so they could enter the furnace and gather the gold nuggets. When inside, one would pick the nuggets up off of the floor and put them into a container. However, without warning, the person was sucked into a vent at the back of the furnace and spit out. He was then required to put the gold he collected into a community pot that would eventually be divided equally between the participants. Then he would give his suit to the next person who in turn went through the same routine. When I awoke, I asked the Lord for understanding of this dream.

The Lord told me that when people realize they have to go through the fire before they can be trusted with the treasure, they promptly put on their fireproof suit, tiptoe around the coals, and quickly grab whatever treasure they can fit in their little basket. They attempt to escape relatively unscathed by the flames. But the Father's furnace spits them out empty-handed and mad at Him because He didn't give them what they wanted – a shortcut to the treasure without truly going through the fire. But wearing a protective suit doesn't count with God. The whole point of the fire is to be raw and repentant before Him and to let Him burn away all those things that hinder us so we can be purified and free. Only then can we be trusted with the treasures of heaven. It's only when we are emptied of ourselves and can stand before Him with empty hands that He can fill us with the riches of His heart.

If we have any hope of entering into deeper intimacy with our Father, we must walk in the valley of the refining fire. Some call it the desert, some call it the fire, most call it lonely and torturous, but God calls it necessary. The burning away of our fleshly desires, or suffering, produces perseverance and character, or reverence, which results in wisdom and a tender intimacy with the Lord. We are greatly mistaken if we expect intimacy without the fire. No fire…no wisdom. "For with much wisdom comes much sorrow; the more knowledge, the more grief," Ecclesiastes 1:18.

What exactly is this fire? After we have acknowledged Jesus as our Savior and have given Him permission to be Lord of our life we are called a "new creation." That means we are no longer bound by the sinful nature that was birthed in the Garden of Eden when Adam and Eve sinned. We are now "adopted" into the DNA of Jesus because of His death on the cross where He took our sin and defeated satan. However, our flesh still wants to have control of our mind and spirit, and a fight breaks out between this flesh and the new Spirit within us. From my experience, it can get pretty ugly. This tension, or fight, is what I call "the furnace" or "fire." It's that place within us that doesn't quite want to let go of our old nature that thrives on earthly pleasures: gossip, lies, pride, selfishness, drugs, alcohol, excess, perversion or anything else that goes against the purity and holiness that we were created for. The "fire" is the process of refinement.

When diamonds are mined, they have to be subjected to excessive heat and pressure before they shine and reflect the true brilliance within. Our rebellious nature, or flesh, has to be brought into submission as we slowly begin to let go of all the enticements and trappings that seemed so good to us at the time. We begin to learn humility, love, and honesty. We start to let go of our former self-centered behavior and slowly start to teach our flesh that it must treat others with respect and dignity just as we want to be treated. We are not a two-year-old anymore and we must let go of two-year-old behavior.

Inviting Jesus into our heart is only the beginning. Yes, the "old man" is now gone, and we are new creations. "Therefore, if anyone is in Christ, he is a new creation; the old has gone, the new has come," 2 Corinthians 5:17. In my life, this "fight" appears as allowing God daily to search my heart and convict me – not condemn – but bring to my attention those areas with wrong motives, pride, or rebellion. It is because I love Jesus and am truly grateful for the price He paid on the cross for my salvation that I go through this fire. I do not want to grieve Him or bring disgrace to His name. It is not easy being humble. It means not always having to "be right" even when I am. When I let the fire "burn away" my flesh it causes me to be more compassionate and loving, even when I don't feel like it. Sometimes it means I won't always get what I want when I want it. I don't usually give my kids candy before lunch. It's not because I don't love them, but because I do love them, and sometimes I have to say no for their own good.

    I'm in the fire now. I'm being stretched and refined. I have to let go of what I want and accept God's will for me over my own. Some days it's bearable, some days it's uneventful, and some days I am reduced to a puddle begging for mercy. A friend of mine recently said, "Just when you think you can't endure another minute, breakthrough is at the door." Another friend, who has walked through significant fires, encouraged me to hold fast to hope. Don't give up. At times I have a propensity to whine and complain, but we all must endure trials. "Consider it pure joy, my brothers, whenever you face trials of many kinds," James 1:2. It's not easy letting go of our fleshly desires. Sometimes God has to pry our fingers off things that are bad for us before we self-destruct! These friends have modeled the art of surviving the fire with grace and dignity, and I can only hope to follow in their footsteps and endure with half as much wisdom and humility as they have. We are in this together, and we need to reach out and lift one another through the hot coals, offering a cold glass of water and God's grace and mercy in abundance.

    Is the fire worth it? Absolutely! It's painful, but it results in the most beautiful fruit. The peace and trust that come are sweet. Intimacy with your Heavenly Father is priceless. One glimpse of the inner court and you are hooked. It's like eating hot dogs and then tasting prime rib – at that moment, you realize somebody's been holding out on you, and there's no going back. Through the fire, I have found the sweetest fellowship with my Daddy. Most importantly, I have found His heart. Although I'll never claim perfection or that I have it all together, I have found such comfort in laying down my own desires and running after my Daddy's heart. Yes, I may still sometimes yell at my husband, or let my mind go to places it has no business going, but I am a work in progress. I am becoming more and more real. My Heavenly Father knows me, He sees me, and His grace is enough.

Is it worth it? Remember the ladies all over my floor? As this group of undone women slowly gathers around the dinner table, still quiet and reflective, we begin what is the first of many meals together. Any pretense has been burned away by this tender time with our Father. What originally started as a women's prayer meeting (advertised as short, and to the point, one hour only) has become hours of sweet time of seeking the heart of God together and ending in communion and a meal. There are no "Marthas" here. We ladle our soup from a pot on the stove, grab a biscuit off the counter, and fill our own glasses. Our communion is simple. The crumbly biscuit is the broken body, a bottle of wine is in the middle of the table, and as we pour our own, we remember the One whom this is all about. We spend the next hour talking about God, asking questions and searching scripture. Nobody wants to go home.

Finally, one by one we say our goodbyes, and they brave the cold as they head home with full tummies and even fuller hearts. We all agree that, like the movie Groundhog Day, we wouldn't mind waking up every day to more of the same.

9

The Narrow Road

I love what the firewalkers have had to teach us. It's all about the journey. It can be difficult and it can be sweet, but the road will always lead us to the heart of our Father and His perfect destiny for each one. There is another road we will travel on this journey also. It is called the "narrow road." Like the firewalkers on their journey, this road will test and refine us. It won't be easy, but our Father will always be right there with us, and it too, will take us to that place of deeper intimacy. Join me as I explore this road of sweet refining.

Do you ever wonder how you got to where you are? Sometimes I can't help but wonder if my path has had more detours than necessary. Despite the growth and many victories the Lord has allowed, I still feel like a slow learner, and it seems that every time I turn around I am on some kind of winding path full of boulders and brush. How did I manage to get so far off course again? One day, I am feeling confident that I'm on the right road, hearing from my Daddy and enjoying life, and the next day I'm cutting through a jungle of vines entangling me, trying to avoid quicksand at every turn. As we pursue who we are, the road of faith and trust can become a seemingly impossible path to navigate. How does that happen?

What do we do when the already narrow road begins to turn into a barely discernible path that begins to be scattered with thorn bushes and rocks and the trees become so dense that we can barely see two feet in front of us? Where do we turn when that almost invisible path begins to twist and turn and we realize we are winding uphill, and finding it harder to breathe on a path that is now almost unrecognizable? Do we stop? Do we press on? We realize we're lost. It's getting dark and we feel alone. We begin to despair, and a feeling rises in the pit of our stomachs wishing we had never started this journey in the first place. The narrow road is scary and uncertain. It will take a supernatural trust and faith to continue.

Walking the narrow road of faith actually means avoiding the wide road of status quo. When I started on this journey as an excited newcomer, I was giddy and naïve. Like most of the world, I believed we were put on this earth to be satisfied and pampered. We don't intentionally set out to believe this – it's just that everywhere we turn there are ways to indulge every craving and pleasure we desire. Food, drink, sex, drugs, toys, boats, cars – whatever we want is ours for the taking. The wide road is full of billboards announcing these delicacies at every exit. Like a rat poised to grab the cheese from the trap, we are totally ignorant of what's about to snap shut on our heads! It looks pretty good from where we stand. What's wrong with a little indulgence? Well, nothing…but while a little cheese is healthy; it's the trap you have to watch out for. Satan loves to bait the trap and entice us.

Before I met the Lord, my wide road was inundated with pleasure. It was strewn with empty beer cans, drugs, parties and basically whatever caught my attention at the time. As the garbage piled up, I just stepped over it and kept going. The Lord allowed me to travel this path for a long time before He said "Enough!" When you have a long way to fall you realize just how much grace you have received. Even when we're too busy satisfying our every whim to take a second glance at our Father, His eye is ever on us and He pursues us relentlessly.

Dear one, we have a choice to make and the stakes are high. The "cheese" may look harmless enough, but one day that trap is going to snap shut on our pretty little head. Our enemy's strategy is to make us so "fat" and over-indulged that we don't notice the stakes growing higher and higher. If we think we can fool ourselves into blindly following every doctrine, indulge in every pleasure, and call what is good evil and what is evil good, we need to stop and take off the blinders. "Woe to those who call evil good and good evil, who put darkness for light and light for darkness," Isaiah 5:20.

I'm not going to sugar coat it. The narrow road isn't easy. It takes hard work, and remember that furnace I talked about? It's right in the middle of the road. In fact, the narrower the road, the more flesh gets left in the ditch. So, why would we want to choose this narrow, difficult, painful path? Why wouldn't we? One very wide, enticing road leads to death and destruction. One very narrow, seemingly difficult path leads to Jesus. We can take the wide road I call "worldly" for a good time and reap death and destruction, or we can opt for the narrow road (Jesus) and we can reap an eternity of "feasting" with the One who can satisfy our every desire – with no hangover in the morning!

Like me, there are many who have had little interest in that narrow road because I was too consumed with enjoying earthly pleasures. Maybe you are there now. It seems pretty fun doesn't it? What's the harm? Life goes on and you're happy and nobody is getting hurt, right? You may be thinking, "God is kind and all good people go to heaven, so lighten up. I'm sick of those Christians harping at me about God and heaven and going to church. And, seriously, the way they fight and bicker and carry on, why would I want to be one of them?" Honestly, I couldn't understand why anyone cared what I was doing or why I did it. And why did they keep talking to me about this man named Jesus? Where was He when I needed Him? Where was He when I was in that dark night of my soul, sinking deeper and deeper into the pit?

Here's what I've learned. You may not "feel" Him with you right now, and you might not think He cares. You may have cursed Him and told Him off, and you might be mad as heck because He hasn't rescued you from whatever circumstances have you down in that slimy pit. Trust me; I've been there many times. Life can feel lonely and unfair, and we're all looking for someone to blame. But there's another force at work: something called free will. God has given us all the gift of choice. He doesn't want robots; He is a gentleman and will never force Himself on anyone. He loves us enough to give us the option of knowing Him, or not.

There's also this crazy law of nature that says we reap what we sow. Sowing simply means planting. If you plant good seed (faithfulness, humility, selflessness), you reap, or receive, a good crop. If you sow bad seed (selfishness, indulgence, pride, a life away from God) you reap a bad crop. "Do not be deceived: God cannot be mocked. A man reaps what he sows. The one who sows to please his sinful nature, from that nature will reap destruction; the one who sows to please the Spirit, from the Spirit will reap eternal life," Galatians 6:7-8.

Of course, there are countless innocent victims that have reaped the ugliness that others have sown. It isn't fair, and we cannot understand why God doesn't intervene and protect the innocent. This age-old question is a hard one to answer; I only know that God is good, and every single one of us has to go before God the Judge, and justice will prevail in the end. I know that God hears the hearts of the innocent cry out. I also know that we don't have to spend the rest of our lives being victims. Even that is a choice. Our Daddy aches to redeem us and free us from those chains made of our wounds that have wrapped so tightly around our necks. It is only the lies that the enemy whispers into our ears that keep us bound. Our heavenly Father can and will free us if we ask Him. We must allow Him to wrap His arms around us and restore our brokenness. I have had my share of wounds; more than once I had that child-like innocence stolen. The scars from that theft run deep. I know the pain, but I also know the freedom. The Jesus that people tried to tell me about…they knew something that I didn't! *

I once described it long ago to my then unbelieving husband this way: "If you were in a burning building, I would do everything in my power to drag you out, even if you were kicking and screaming and fighting me every step of the way. I wouldn't worry about hurting your feelings. I wouldn't try to be politically correct. I would forget about my limitations, throw you over my shoulder, and drag you out of that burning building."

If you haven't invited Jesus to be Lord of your life, you are headed for that "burning building." Believe me; you will be pretty mad at those people who decided not to hurt your feelings by not pushing that Jesus guy on you! Take the time to think about this; your eternity is at stake. I prayed for my husband for twenty years before he invited Jesus to be Lord of his life. It was a long journey but now we walk united, truly as one, with Christ as the head. Our eternity is secure, not because of anything we do, but because of what Jesus did.

People will often point an angry finger at God and blame Him for their mess of a life. But the truth is, He is good. He cares and is always watching and waiting for us to turn to Him. Don't tell me He doesn't care when He protected me and others when I drove drunk, when at parties we would dare each other to sit in the middle of the road at the bottom of a hill on a very busy highway, when I was promiscuous, when I took drugs, when I woke up not knowing where I was, or a million other times that I was just plain stupid. I took that wide road for many years, and He kept me through it all.

As that lonely child, I would sit in a field by my home and ask, "Is there anybody up there?" "Will anyone ever love me?" I had no idea that my Daddy was there and would protect me through all the stupid choices I would make. I had no clue He already had a wonderful man to be my husband who would indeed love me, and that there were beautiful children and grandchildren in my future. He knew all the stupid things I would do and all the ugliness that I would sow! There are always consequences for our choices and sometimes they will follow us well into our life, but when we turn to God, they no longer keep us from His love.

Just as now, if I eat sugar or gluten, I will be VERY sick – it's my choice! One choice will have good consequences and one will not. God will not love me any more or any less, but one choice will not end well for me. Back when I was making very bad choices, God didn't look at me and say, "Wow, I didn't see that coming." Yet He loved me enough to protect me through it all and accept me when I came running into His arms. All I had to do was tell Him I was sorry and that I didn't want to be on that ugly road anymore. That's it. No condemnation, no lectures, no making me beg and plead and no more lost soul.

So, when you're ready to hop off that road, just call on Jesus' name, and He will be there. He has been there all along. It may take some time and effort on your part to recover from those wounds, but you will never be sorry. Please trust me. Please don't wait too long. We never know when our short time here on earth will come to an abrupt end, and if you were my friend I would do everything in my power to drag you out of that burning building, even if it meant offending you.

And about those Christians who aren't perfect: you're right. Christians aren't perfect; they're just forgiven. They're imperfect. That's why we need Jesus. He offers us complete freedom from our past and freedom for our future. Let's run after His offer with everything we've got. Lay down your pride, open your heart and take a chance on Jesus. He won't let you down. He never does! "Keep your lives free from the love of money and be content with what you have, because God has said, 'Never will I leave you; never will I forsake you.'" Heb. 13:5.

10

Milk or Meat?

Can I meddle for a minute? Would you consider yourself a good Christian? Do you say a quick prayer over your food and ask Jesus to bless you and "keep your soul till you wake?" Do you go to church on Sundays and Wednesdays and bring Jell-O and a large tuna casserole to potlucks? Do you know the hymns by heart and get upset when some "punks" try to convert to contemporary music just because they think the hymns are too "old fashioned?" I mean, we have always done it this way, and it works, so why change a good thing?

Sometimes we fall into a rut of thinking that since God is the same yesterday, today and tomorrow, we should be too. Most of us don't like change – myself included! But after some pretty intense encounters with God, change might as well be my middle name! My days used to be comfortable and quiet. I was walking out the typical Christian life, and on a Richter scale of one to ten, most of the time there wasn't much shaking going on. Just an occasional tremor from time to time…but then…God happened!

Have you ever had that experience? You thought you would spend the rest of your life in your nice little church in your same little pew with your same little friends. You would stay in your same little neighborhoods, same dog, same cat, same hymns, and same prayers. Comfortable and cozy in the world that we know, it's hard to be open to change. But we are meant to live constantly changing lives. Nowhere in scripture did anyone ever stay comfortable and change their world! Yes, we can choose to stay in the comfortable life we've created, but I guarantee that after three thousand Jell-O's and tuna casseroles you will be bored to tears and your eulogy will read like a cookbook.

I really don't want to have this conversation with Jesus: "What did you do with your time on earth?" "Well I perfected green Jell-O with cabbage, and I could whip up the best tuna salad in the county. I knew every hymn by heart, I got all those young know-it-alls kicked out of the church on their ear, and I served on every committee that was available. I knew the church constitution by heart and I made sure it was followed to the letter. I prayed over every meal and memorized the Ten Commandments. I made sure everyone knew when a trespass was committed by one of those 'sinners,' of course so we could pray for them, and I made sure the pastor knew all about the family of those kids who came to our youth group. You know, the ones whose parents would drop them off and then go to the bar…"

I so wish I could laugh with you at that lady, but sadly, that lady was me. As I look back at that woman who thought she was the most faithful, godly woman in the church, it doesn't seem quite so funny to me anymore. I thought I was doing the right thing by performing the right rituals, being the "good" Christian, obeying the right rules and setting such a fine example. In truth, I was like the Pharisees. I had that rulebook so tightly in my grasp that I couldn't see the chains that had me tangled up in their nice little web of deception.

Have you ever watched a spider weave its web so perfectly and intricately? It is methodical. The web looks so innocent. It's hard to believe it could become such a trap. Well, a trap it is, and it is woven with the sole purpose of being a trap. It may look pretty, and shimmer in the sunshine, but once you venture too close, it's all over. Once you are stuck in the sticky strands, you are at the mercy of the spider. It may not eat you right away, it may let you squirm and even lull you into a false sense of security. You might even start to feel comfortable and start thinking this isn't so bad after all. But sooner or later the spider goes in for the kill. That's what our enemy likes to do, he likes to lull us into a false sense of security and let us get comfortable. Pretty soon we begin to forget that we are even in a trap. We just get comfortable and settle in; we admire the view. The web looks kind of pretty, seems well made and the intricate design is interesting. Nobody is rocking my boat. Nobody is challenging me or pressing me too hard to grow or change or "get out of my comfort zone." It's all just business as usual. Don't rock the boat; leave well enough alone.

That's where I was…until my God-tsunami hit! It all happened so quickly that at first I wasn't sure what was even happening. I innocently picked up a book called "Anything" by Jennie Allen.[2] If you haven't read this book I urge you to pray seriously and count the cost first. Until then, I honestly had not even thought about the words "count the cost." Up until then, there hadn't really been much of a cost so I thought the whole shaking stuff was the imaginings of delirious people. What little I knew of my Daddy could have fit in a small salt shaker used to spice my spiritual food now and then when I felt like it. I kept my pew warm, served for funerals, and served on a circuit of committees. I visited the sick, dressed all pretty with all my bling, and said the right things. Let me be clear: there is nothing inherently wrong with these things. These all have to be done, and I have the highest respect for the people who do them; they are saints. My heart and gratitude go to the ladies of the church who faithfully serve and teach and have taken me under their wings and nurtured me while I was in my Christian high chair sipping my bottle of milk.

But, God made us for more, and He wasn't about to let me spend the rest of my life in that baby chair. As comfortable as it was, it wasn't productive. It wasn't fulfilling my destiny. He began creating a hunger in me that grew into a full blown insatiable spiritual appetite. Milk just wasn't filling me anymore, and I started hunting for solid food like a maniac. I devoured everything I could get my hands on and

Can I Just be Real?

made everyone around me crazy with question after question! I questioned everything! Nothing was safe. Everything I had ever learned suddenly had to be reviewed and analyzed and put under the God microscope. My poor pastor once told me I was "a burr in his saddle." I'm pretty sure people would duck into the nearest closet when they saw me coming. Remember the first time you ever ate a perfectly cooked juicy steak or shrimp or lobster smothered in butter? Did it make you want to run right out and eat a hot dog? NO! It made you want more of the good stuff! That's what God does to us. Once we have a real encounter with Him we can't go back, it's just not possible.

Have you ever had a God encounter that made you say, "Anything?" Did God show up and leave you breathless or awestruck or just plain speechless? I can't say I was really looking for it or even when it exactly happened. There wasn't one big defining moment. It was more of a hunger that just began to grow and became more and more intense until I couldn't ignore it any more. I wanted to know God more! And when you set out on a quest to know God more, He will show you everything you want to know, and a whole lot of what you didn't even know to ask. In total ignorance, I said those infamous words, "Anything, God. I will do anything You ask." It was out of my hunger that I told God I didn't want life as usual anymore. I knew I was created for more: more of Him, more of me, and more of life. I didn't know there would be a cost, but I can honestly say that the cost is so worth it. The cost is allowing God to renew us into His image. Our flesh screams and whines, and sometimes it gets ugly! Our flesh wants what our flesh wants. Our world tells us that we SHOULD get what we want when we want it. Why simmer when you can microwave? The culture encourages us to be selfish and self-indulgent.

Remember when I talked about the furnace? The furnace is being willing to allow God to burn away all that ugly flesh that was birthed out of the infamous garden where sin began. God did not mean for it to be this way, but we went astray and chose life apart from Him. We bought into the lie of the snake, and "flesh" was created. That sinful nature that screams to be noticed and fed now competes with the God-nature in us that longs to transform us into the image of Christ, bringing purity and holiness. I chose to jump into that furnace because I love Jesus way more than I love my flesh and I want that flesh burned up and gone.

On this journey of life, we learn who we are and who we are not. Part of maturing, growing and refining is the "meat" that scripture refers to. "Solid food is for the mature, who by constant use have trained themselves to distinguish good from evil," Hebrews 5:14. Along with the word "anything" must come the prayer, "You are the vine and I am only a branch, apart from You I can do nothing," (adapted from John 15:5). We cannot walk this life apart from Christ. The Lord has asked me to do things that I couldn't possibly do without Him. He has asked me to speak in front of people which used to terrify me. He has asked me to take on leadership roles which go against every ounce of my being. He guides me as I learn how to be a better friend and wife and how to be more honest and open. He holds my hand as I navigate the ups and downs of deeper trust and faith. He has proven that if I trust Him even when nothing makes sense, He will take care of me.

Several years ago, the Lord told my husband and me that He would provide for us just as He did for Elijah at the brook, one day at a time. "The ravens brought him bread and meat in the morning and bread and meat in the evening, and he drank from the brook," 1 Kings 17:6. Now, on paper our expenses exceed our income, yet we have never missed a payment, and we tithe and sow seeds generously. We don't worry about money, and we don't chase the American dream. Our lives are simple, yet full and rich. We speak truth that isn't always popular, and we have lost friends because of it. The Lord has taught us to be less selfish and more forgiving. It is a tough thing to be unoffendable; our flesh would want us to be angry, hold grudges, be slow to forgive, and keep account of wrongs. Even small things, like just wanting a little bit more than we have, can take our focus off who we are and Who can make us happy. Our flesh clamors for wealth and fame, always wanting more. If I just had this job, or that house, or someone said this, or paid more attention to me. If my spouse did this or if I just lost a few more pounds…it's a merry-go-round way of thinking. Our happiness becomes one more thing just out of reach. It eludes us like a gold ring that is dangling in front of us. If we could only stretch out far enough to grab it! It continually entices us to work harder and longer because any minute it will be ours. Then we can kick back and enjoy our bounty. Yet, we never quite get there; it's always just inches from our grasp. That's what the refining is all about. It adjusts our focus from us to Him. We learn Who He is and what's important to Him. We learn that it's truly about Him – not about us. The secret to always having your prayers answered is to ask the Father what His will is and then pray it back to Him.

    I confess, I've had to learn the hard way, just like I always do. I was once so mad at God because my prayers weren't answered the way I wanted, that I actually threw my Bible across the room, which was followed by my glasses. I then let loose with a tantrum that would make a two-year-old blush. I didn't always like the answers He gave – I still don't. But part of maturing is asking His will, accepting it, and praying accordingly. I have prayed for very ill friends only to have my Daddy tell me that He is taking them home, and no amount of begging would change that fact. It is hard to reconcile my mind to understand that while Jesus heals and it is His desire for all to be healed, not all are. Other times I have petitioned and He has said "yes" before the words were even out of my mouth. We have to understand that His ways are not our ways, and no matter how hard we try, we won't always understand things that happen in this life. Life is not fair, but God is fair and just. We don't have to always understand, we just need to listen, pray and trust. I have learned to first ask how to pray and then pray. Jesus said that He only did what His Father did and only said what His Father said – Period! "For whatever I say is just what the Father has told me to say," John 12:50. He did not interject His own will or make plans and then expect His Father to bless them. Jesus spent time alone with His Father, found out what His will was, and then did it.

Hearing the Lord's voice is exciting, and learning to chew the harder meat of life is rewarding and filling, but we can still get tripped up on wrong thinking. Sometimes I think I am so important that everyone's well-being hinges on me. I think that if someone gets hurt or sick, it's because I didn't pray long enough or at all. If prayers aren't answered the way I want, it's because I didn't say the right words or pray correctly. I think that He would hear me better if only I knew how to pray more effectively or eloquently. What if I woke up earlier, or stayed up later, or knew more scripture? Maybe if I had gone to seminary, or had the gift…then God would have answered me. We trust God when He says "yes," but doubt Him when He says "no." I love this quote by Oswald Chambers: "Faith is not a bargain with God – I will trust you if you give me money, but not if you don't. We have to trust in God whether He sends us money or not, whether He gives us health or not. We must have faith in God, not in His gifts. Let us walk before God and be perfect, you in your circumstances and I in mine; then we will prove ourselves true children of Abraham."[3]

Sometimes meat is hard to digest. It can be wonderful, but it can also be tough and sometimes needs to be chewed for a long time before it can be swallowed. I still would rather have meat than milk, but sometimes I have to have someone cut it up for me into bite-sized pieces so I don't choke on it. Jesus spoke a lot in parables because He wanted us to dig for the hidden treasure in His words. He knew we needed more than milk; he wanted us to grow teeth and learn to chew. I have a new puppy, and he chews relentlessly on everything. His teeth are sharp because he uses them ALL the time. I want sharp spiritual teeth, which to me translates as wisdom, so I can digest truths even if they are hard to swallow. The only place I can get that wisdom is at my Father's feet.

I will never pretend to have it all together or have all the answers. Sometimes I don't even feel close to getting that ugly flesh out of the way. But I do know that I would NEVER turn back, even through the pain of being weaned off of milk. I have grown in my walk with my Daddy. He's taught me how to chew the meat and be nourished by it. I love Him in ways that I didn't even know were possible. I love having conversations with Him, I love His nature, His sense of humor, His beauty, His kindness, His creativity, His Holiness, His mercy …there is seriously no end to our Daddy's nature. It just goes on and on forever. I can't even imagine what it will be like seeing Him face to face, but I can and do talk with Him every day. I ask questions, laugh, nag, petition, contend, laugh, and ponder with my Daddy. He is amazing! One of my husband's favorite sayings is, "Every day is a school day."

Friend, we are on a journey. Each day our Father makes Himself available to us, if only we ask. He wants to walk and talk with us and teach us. It is my prayer that you will NEVER again be content with the milk of life, but that you will hunger for the meat. I pray that you will begin a journey with an insatiable appetite for more of Him each day. Don't allow yourself to be content where you are. You were made for so much more. Dear one, you are a child of the Most High God, Creator of the Universe. You have the mind of Christ, and you are beautiful in every way. You are a diamond waiting to come out of that furnace more beautiful than you could ever imagine. Don't wait another day. Count the cost, chew the meat, swallow hard, have some chocolate for courage and say it: "Anything, God!"

11

Talk is Cheap

Martha, if I were with you in the kitchen I would say "show me" a lot. Forget the cookbook and those ridiculously long directions; just teach me how to knead the bread and baste the lamb and fold the napkins. I learn better by example versus those lengthy instruction novels. Are you good at reading instructions? Do you have one of those engineer minds where you can reason and fix anything or assemble things faster than I could get the directions unfolded? Aren't you special!

Every time I hear a sermon or a teaching, I am left with one question, "What does that look like?" Does anyone else do that? It all sounds so good, but how do we walk it out every day in real life? What does it look like to have an intimate relationship with our Father? What does it look like to be transformed into the image of Jesus? How long is long enough to be in my prayer closet? Where is my prayer closet? I've heard of mothers whose prayer closet is an apron pulled up over their head. Picture a mom with a whole litter of kids with runny noses and dirty diapers running around squealing and pulling the cat's tail and demanding milk and cookies, the puppy peeing on the floor, and dishes piled to the ceiling. Going to the bathroom alone is completely wishful thinking! (Sorry, just reminiscing for a moment.) A quiet, peaceful prayer closet – yeah right!

So even as I'm writing, I am asking myself if I'm explaining how to get to where we are going or am I just painting a picture of the scenery along the way? I wish I had the answers to all these questions, but just when I think I might actually have it figured out, another layer of the spiritual "onion" is peeled away, and I am left back at square one again. God is just so big and my mind is, well, so small! My mind wanders like a nomad in the desert. How many times can one person lose their glasses? And then when you finally find them on top of your head you try to act all normal like you knew they were there all along. I once tried to stuff a full gallon of milk in the cupboard with my cups and got crazy mad when it wouldn't fit. Why would I do that? Because the lights were on but nobody was home! My mind was on a sand dune somewhere wandering around with the tumbleweeds. Please don't tell me I'm the only one that does these things, I'm insecure enough. At least humor me so I don't feel so, shall I say...woefully inept.

What do we do with all these questions floating around making us wonder if we are the only ones in the universe who don't have an answer? Let's revisit something I said earlier. How many of you feel that you don't hear God speak to you? Well, listen up. I know my Daddy also happens to be your Daddy. The Man is deliriously crazy about you, and He is not playing some cosmic hide and seek. "Ask, and it will be given to you; seek and you will find; knock and the door will be opened to you. For everyone who asks receives; he who seeks finds; and to him who knocks, the door will be opened," John 7:7-8.

ASK! I may have mentioned earlier that some of my friends have been quite verbal about my nagging skills. If God says, "ASK," I ask. I understand that you may feel like you are talking to a brick wall, and you don't feel God answers YOUR prayers. You may feel way too sinful to talk to Him. You might not think He listens to you so why should you waste your time? You might wonder sometimes if it's really Him talking to you or if it's just your imagination or even satan? You may not think you hear Him like others do. You might question why He would talk to you. I'm not going to give you a lot of scripture here, but God does say, "Which of you, if his son asks for bread will give him a stone?" John

7:9. Listen closely: God is perched on the edge of His seat waiting for you to talk to Him. He wants so badly for you to find Him and talk to Him that He will chase you to the ends of the earth. He will wipe away your every tear, erase your every transgression if you ask, and He will lavish love on you like you're the most amazing person on the planet. Because to Him, you are!

SEEK! Did you ever play hide and seek as a child? You know – "One, two, skip a few, ninety nine, one hundred. Ready or not here I come." Did you just look behind one bush and then give up? I bet not. Children are curious and tenacious. They don't like to lose. I used to play the game with my kids at night in our big yard, but the dog always followed me and gave me away. God will hide in plain sight or cough or sneeze just so you can find Him. If you feel like you are seeking too hard, then just sit quietly for a while. Before you know it, your eyes will adjust to the dark, and you will see Him right there in front of you. You can throw your head back and laugh and run into His arms and hug the stuffing out of Him while He does the same. Sometimes what keeps us from seeing Him is our own stubbornness, blindness or pride. Pride is a BIG blindfold! Remember the flesh? The flesh LOVES to think it has everything under control and doesn't need anybody else, especially God. I want to be independent and "strong" and NEVER stop to ask for directions.

God hates pride. He loves us, but He hates our pride. Pride will make us do things that distance us from our Father. Holiness and pride cannot dwell together, so when pride takes over He has to take a step back and wait for us to run back into His arms. The best way to deal with pride is to repent immediately, accept His forgiveness and tell that devil to take a hike. I ask the Lord quite often to "create in me a pure heart and keep me from willful sin," Psalm 51:10. That's part of that "furnace" I talked about. The biggest role we play is being moldable and humble, and willing to admit mistakes. Take responsibility for your actions, bring them before God's throne, accept forgiveness, and not do it again. We ALL make mistakes, sin, stumble over our own feet and mess up. God knows we have a sinful nature. He cares about what we do after we sin. When we try to cover it up or ignore it, then it just sits there like a big boil getting more infected by the day. Sooner or later it's going to blow, and it won't be pretty; we might as well just acknowledge it and deal with it.

KNOCK! What would happen if you knocked on your neighbor's door at one in the morning? Well, it depends on the neighbor, but chances are he wouldn't be very happy. Unless it's an emergency, you better think twice and at least have a plate of warm chocolate chip cookies in your hand. Guess what? God is up all night! You can knock any time, day or night, 24/7. You don't even need warm cookies, an excuse, or an emergency. You can just knock and He will answer. Not only will He answer, but He will invite you in and stay up all night talking to you, comforting you or just hanging out. He has no expectations of you, won't nag, will lovingly stare at you like you ARE a chocolate chip cookie, and He will listen to your every care and concern and never once yawn or be bored. He's such a Daddy that way!

We are His little children, and He is our big strong Daddy. His home is always open. Let me put it this way – as a parent, my children and their families have legal access to me, my home and all that belongs to me at any time. Even though they are grown, they are still welcome to walk into my house, open the fridge and help themselves to anything they want. Our son knows his dad's garage is full of tools that are available to him at any time. Everything we have is available to them; they don't have to beg or plead or stand outside in the rain. They can just walk in and act like they are at home. Why? Because they carry our DNA and they have a legal right and our permission. Are you getting the picture? That's the way it is with our Heavenly Father.

We carry His DNA and He has given us access to everything He is and has. We don't have to beg and plead and stand outside in the rain. He has already invited us in and told us we are His heirs, His children, princes and princesses, sons and daughters! "If we are [God's] children, then we are heirs – heirs of God and co-heirs with Christ, if indeed we share in His sufferings in order that we may also share in His glory," Romans 8:17. Obviously, I want my children to treat me with respect, and in return, I will treat them with respect. If they have a need I will do all in my power to help them. When they hurt, I hurt. When they cry, I cry. When they rejoice, I rejoice. When they were young and naughty, I would discipline them and then tell them how much I loved them. If they knock on my door asking for bread, I will give them the whole loaf. Why? Because I love them. If we ask our Daddy, seek His face and knock on His door, He WILL answer. Why? Because He loves us!

If you want answers, if you want to hear His voice, if you want joy and love and forgiveness, ask, seek, and knock. Ask until you get answers. Seek and don't give up. Knock and then enter. It may take practice to hear His voice and know it's His voice, but it WILL happen. Ask Him to teach you. Don't forget to listen. Sometimes He whispers and we have to be very quiet to be able to hear. Other times His voice will thunder and you will know in your Spirit that it is Him. He may speak through His Word, a book, a magazine, a gentle nudging, or a "knowing." Sometimes He speaks through others or songs or poems. He's a master at creativity, so be ready and open. If you're not sure, ask Him to confirm.

Ask, seek, and knock. How much easier could it be? Give it a try. You might just find that you have a Heavenly Father who is crazy in love with you and will fling that door wide open. You may even discover He has a fridge full of the best treats ever just for you!

12

Life is Messy Get Used to it

I have a five-month-old Shih Tzu puppy named Jake. Yes, he is adorable, and yet, anyone who's owned a puppy is probably nodding their heads with understanding and feeling very sorry for me. Every place we go people stop and want to pet him and take him home. Some days I wouldn't think twice about letting someone take him home, and some days I would even pay someone to take him home. Puppies are stubborn! Puppies are like the Tasmanian devil on steroids! We just had our carpets professionally cleaned about six months before we got our lovable little guy. I'm sure if the cleaner saw them right now he would be mortified! He would probably cry and beg us not to tell a soul that he was the one that did the job! I want to cry myself; what was I thinking?

Animal lovers are strange people. They will put up with stained carpet, messes everywhere, and fur balls sweeping across the floor like tumbleweeds. The whimpering and whining (and that's just me), going outside a million times a day, grooming, combing, trips to the vet, chewing…well, you get the picture! At my age I have owned enough animals to know very well the patience and perseverance it takes, but I also know the reward. When they climb up on your lap and bury their little faces in your neck and fall asleep, it's so precious and sweet. They are like kids really. They can make you insane, but when they are sleeping you forget the insanity and just see how cute they are. It makes you feel so warm and fuzzy. The difference between animals and kids is that you can put the animals in a cage without going to prison!

Can I Just be Real?

Life with the Lord is kind of like owning a puppy or kitten or monkey or whatever you choose to be crazy enough to share your home with. The idea itself is all rainbows and sunshine. You don't really realize the messiness that will come. It sounds really good, and it is, but even Jesus says that He didn't come so we could be lazy and kick back on the couch and never deal with any messes. Please don't get me wrong – I would NOT trade my life with Jesus for twenty lives without Him, but I think sometimes we are mistakenly told that once we accept Jesus as Lord, everything will be all soft, purring kittens from then on...Soft kitty, warm kitty, little ball of fur. Happy kitty, sleepy kitty, purr, purr, purr! I don't know about you but it all sounds so good to me – the easy part that is. I am practically comatose when I can curl up in the warm sunshine with a soft animal and sleep.

Speaking of soft animals, a bear just casually wandered across my yard to grab a drink out of our rain barrel. We also have a mama fox and three babies living under our shed, deer running rampant across our yard, bunnies, skunks, an occasional porcupine wandering through, and whatever else decides to scope out the area. That wouldn't be so unusual except we live in town! And remember I have a puppy that needs to go outside pretty much hourly. Mind you when I say I look both ways and double check, I am not talking about watching for cars.

So what does this have to do with Jesus? Besides the fact that I trust Him to protect me from the wild animals when I go outside, and I think He loves babies and animals and that He created us all to co-exist, I think there are some lessons here. I once owned a ferret when my kids were teenagers. I didn't want him or ask for him, but when he showed up at my house I resigned myself to the fact that I was stuck with him. It's kind of like life – trials come to our house even when we don't ask for them, and we don't want them and we could live quite comfortably without them. None of us are exempt. It makes no difference what color we are, what race, religion, nationality or personality. Whether we are thin or not so thin, old, young, city dwellers, country dwellers, cave dwellers – whatever, you get the picture. It's not that God created it this way, but a long time ago in a perfect garden someone got a bit greedy and ate an apple. The rest is history. I'm not throwing stones. If not Eve, I'm sure it would have been me, because even now I tend to hear that familiar hiss in my ears and am tempted to believe a little white lie that knocks me right off my shiny little pedestal. Will I ever learn?

So, here I am minding my own business, snuggling my furry friend and bam! Something gets messy. My "life carpet" used to be stain free (I think maybe when I was still in the womb). Then life happened, and the stains started to accumulate. You know what I mean? Messy little things like pride and selfishness, a little white lie here and there, lust, unforgiveness, envy, anger, trauma, sudden death, an unexpected illness, an accident, betrayal, abuse…the list could go on forever. All of a sudden our world is shaken. We didn't ask for it but it shows up on our doorstep and demands attention. Sometimes, we unwittingly cause the arrival of these trials. For example, two of the biggest spiritual factors that contribute to illness are fear and unforgiveness; they are literally poison to our body. If we hold unforgiveness in our hearts, it will manifest outwardly causing a weakened immune system leaving our physical body prey to infirmity. Fear and worry will do the same. Remember we are body, soul, and spirit and they cannot be separated. Body reacts to soul, soul reacts to spirit, spirit reacts to body, and body reacts to spirit.

So, what do we do with this mess? Good question! We come alongside each other and together we navigate the pitfalls and messes. When a soul is hurting, we remind each other how dearly loved we are by our Heavenly Daddy, and we exhibit that love in the flesh. When our flesh is wounded, we stand in the gap and storm the heavenlies on behalf of one another. When our dear brother or sister is caught in the pain of unforgiveness or fear or worry, we gently come beside them and walk with them through the path of cutting those chains. We go to scripture and study the Living Word together as we allow the sweet work of the Holy Spirit to minister to our wounds and free us from the lies that hold us captive.

Remember what I said earlier about patience and perseverance? We have not yet passed the stage with our puppy Jake where he is more fun than work. We're making progress, but he still tries our patience at times. Yesterday, I had to take our comforter to the laundromat because the day before I had thought it was safe to let Jake snuggle with me on our bed (you saw that writing on the wall, didn't you!). I just sighed and reminded myself that I was pushing my luck just a bit. Did I get mad at him and throw a fit? No. He's a puppy, and I confess, my propensity to laziness got the best of me. I didn't take him outside before we went to bed – my bad. This is a gentle reminder that doing life together isn't always easy, but it's in those messy times that we need to ask the Holy Spirit for extra love and perseverance. We must bear with one another in love just as we would want others to bear with us. "Bear with each other and forgive whatever grievances you may have against one another. Forgive as the Lord forgave you," Colossians 3:13.

Let's face it, life is messy! It's messy for each one of us. It's messy whether we ask for it or are just minding our own business when it blindsides us like a semi-truck out of control. Right now every one of our prayer group ladies is going through some kind of "mess." We have moms with very serious illnesses, court battles, finances, business concerns, personal struggles, and some just trying to keep their heads above water. I dearly love these women! We have made a commitment to each other and to the Lord to come together weekly, bringing our messes and our joys and lay them out on the table. Just a few days ago we were all sitting on my deck enjoying the sunshine and summer breeze as we spoke what was in our hearts. We then went into a sweet time of worship. The stains didn't disappear on the carpet, and situations didn't miraculously change (although God has been known to do that!), but our hearts were soothed. We felt a little lighter as we petitioned the courts of Heaven in the way only "sisters" can do who truly love one another.

You see, it's not about how many stains are on the carpet or how long it takes to "train the puppy" so to speak. It's not about the destination; it's about getting through the journey TOGETHER. It's about leading one another to the throne room and allowing God to refine us and conform us into His image one mess at a time. It's about love and patience and perseverance and lifting one another up when we just can't seem to get our feet under us. When one of us is in distress we send out a text. Within minutes our cell phones start pinging like sonar in a submarine. My daughter once got included in a group text for prayer. She said she almost had to shut her phone off while she was at work because it was "pinging" endlessly. And let me tell you, these are no "sissy" prayers. These people are warriors and they don't go timidly before the throne. We need to go boldly before the throne and make our petitions and requests known. We need to let that hissing snake know that we will step on his head in a heartbeat – not because we are arrogant, but because we have a Father who has given us authority to do so. "I have given you authority to trample on snakes and scorpions and to overcome all the power of the enemy; nothing will harm you," Luke 10:19.

The other day I was at a store at the checkout. The cashier asked me why I was smiling. To be honest, I didn't know why I was smiling. I wasn't having a particularly great day and couldn't think of any good reason offhand. I told her I didn't know why, I just was. She said not many people smile at her and that it was rare to see someone smiling especially for no reason. Sad, isn't it? I wish I would have given some profound "God" wisdom, but all I said was, "Too bad; more people should smile." The lady in line behind me was staring straight ahead and for a minute I was afraid she had been possessed by some kind of zombie and I was in danger of being eaten. When she realized I was looking at her she flashed the fakest smile I had ever seen. One of those all-teeth, ear to ear, "I wish you would mind your own business and leave me alone" kind of smiles. We all three broke out in laughter as she became aware of her expression! As I sat in my car and reflected on that interaction, several thoughts flashed through my mind. I wish I would have talked about God. I should have told them I had the joy of the Lord or how much He loved them or something, anything to bring God into the conversation.

I have a friend who NEVER misses an opportunity to talk about God, and I knew she would have not missed this easy one. Oh well, God wasn't beating me up about it so I decided to put down my own whip. I was taken off guard, and even though scripture says to be prepared in and out of season to give an account of our faith (2 Timothy 4), I missed it. It's not the first time, and I can only hope it will be the last. (Anyone want to make any bets?) The second thing I thought was how sad it was that she had to ask me why I was smiling because so few people do. Maybe she thought I was making fun of her or had a bug in my bra or had been drinking in the parking lot or was planning to drink in the parking lot! I don't know. Maybe, just maybe, the Holy Spirit thought she needed a smile and put one on my face just for her. I hope that is the case. After all she is a "sister" and we are all in this together. Maybe life has been messy for her and maybe just a smile was all she needed. I pray she knows she is loved and that her "Daddy" adores her even in whatever mess she has right now.

My puppy is a work in progress; I am a work in progress; and you are a work in progress. Let's not be too quick to judge or critique one another, especially when we are down. Age has done things to me, and I mean things besides the graying hair (which I color), the wrinkles, sagging and drooping, and progressive "weirdness." I am learning that I need to slow down, not get my big girl undies in a bunch, and relax! The Lord is teaching me about a love that goes so much deeper than skin and a perseverance that makes waiting a bit more bearable. He's given me an ability to look past the stains on others, and maybe just maybe, to work on my own stains first. I am becoming a fierce warrior – not by my own might but simply because love dictates that I pick up my sword and fight for my brothers and sisters with an intensity I have not known before.

I absolutely hate satan. I will go to great lengths these days to make sure he does as little damage as possible to those I love and to ensure that the wounds he has inflicted are healed. I do this by prayer and petition, by taking my rightful position as a child of the Most High God, and claiming my inheritance as that daughter. That means you and I have authority to take back what rightfully belongs to us including our minds, our bodies and our joy! Satan is a thief and a liar! I ask you, dear one, to also pick up your sword, put on your armor (Ephesians 6), and take back every last thing that the devil has stolen from you. We have the mind of Christ; and we need to be using it. If you don't feel you have the strength right now, you are not alone. Some days I can barely get out of bed let alone pick up a sword. Send out an SOS and get your brothers and sisters busy on your behalf. We are not meant to be an island. We are created to be part of a spiritual body and there is a reason for that. When a brother or sister is down we need to get on our faces and begin lifting the wounded to our Heavenly Father and not rest until our answer is sealed. Please be aware, we may not always receive the answer we ask for, but we will always receive the answer that is our Father's good and perfect will. Sometimes we will have to suck it up and be happy with that, He is God after all, and we are not!

As I write this, my little "Jakey" is lying at my feet sleeping and in this moment is the cutest little thing with four paws. His sharp little puppy teeth are put away and his toys are strewn all over the house. The carpet stains are still there but at least for now there are no new ones. The clean comforter is drying on the line, and there is peace. I am heeding the saying not to wake a sleeping giant (or puppy). All too soon we will brave the bears in the yard, dodge the fox and keep our distance from any stray skunks.

My prayer for you is that above all you will know who you are in Christ, and you will live as children of the most High God. I pray you will love unconditionally, fight hard, lean on your brothers and sisters when you need a rest, and forgive at all costs. (That doesn't mean forget or continue in a toxic relationship.) Get yourself surrounded by some strong, godly people and NEVER believe the lies of the enemy! NEVER! Get in the Word and remember who you are!

13

Lay it Down

Do you think Martha was ever lonely? I wonder if she ever felt left out and a little bit "out of sorts." Have you ever felt that way? I wonder if Jesus ever asked her to lay down all she was and did – basically her identity – at His feet and trust Him to fill her empty hands with something better. As I wander the halls of scripture, I realize that most everyone at one time or another had to take a trip to the desert for a time of solitude and dying to self. It's a rite of passage if we have any hope of advancing to a higher level of intimacy, ministry, or balance of any kind.

A while ago, I thought I was in the desert but it turns out I was only at a bus stop next to some cactus. It was a bit hot and thorny but it was only mild preparation for the journey. I'm not sure I have truly hit the real desert yet but it's getting more desolate and arid with each step. Oh dear friend, I have been taken away from so many precious fellowships. Just recently the Lord told me to lay down a ministry that was so close to my heart and dear to me. He told me that just as the Israelites followed the fire by night and the cloud by day, I was to do the same. "God who went ahead of you on your journey, in fire by night and in a cloud by day," Deuteronomy 1:33. When the cloud settled, they were to set up camp and stay until it moved. When it moved, they didn't ask questions, they just had to pack up the tents and follow. "In all the travels of the Israelites, whenever the cloud lifted from above the tabernacle, they would set out; but if the cloud did not lift, they did not set out until it lifted," Exodus 40:37. We can stay, if we want, where the Glory of the Lord has lifted but I don't know why we would want to. When the Lord is no longer in our camp, things get stale. Have you ever seen stagnant water in a shallow pond? If pond water doesn't have an inlet or outlet, it gets green and full of algae and the smell is enough to choke a horse! When the Lord moves, I would rather load up the camels and follow Him than stay and become a breeding ground for dead, stinky stuff.

If I had my choice, I would live someplace very much like Paradise. It would be green, lush, and warm all the time. There wouldn't be mosquitoes or wood ticks and the flowers would be beautiful beyond description. There would be waterfalls cascading into clear pools, with bunnies, puppies, and kittens romping all over the grass while I napped peacefully nearby. No ants would crawl all over me, and I would never have to look over my shoulder for wandering bears. Someday I will be there, but until that time when we are blessed to pass from this world into the next, we still have to navigate this world that is not paradise.

There will be times of peace and beauty for us but there will also be times when we need to go to the desert to have some heart time with our Daddy. We are in good company; Moses had to go as did David, Paul, Elijah and even Jesus. It's where we get alone to hear that still small voice away from the noise and "all that glitters" to compete for our attention. It's where we open our hands to let go of all that is fleshly. We must die so we can really live. Sometimes even "good" ministries must die so they don't become stagnant and start growing scum. It's not easy to walk away, especially when it appears we have hit our stride, and success or breakthrough is so close we can almost reach out and grab it. From out of nowhere the Lord might say "Will you give it to me and walk away?" or "Not yet," or "This season is over," or just simply "No." Your first thought may be, "I'm sure I'm not hearing this right, it can't be." Then, "Lord give me confirmations," and the confirmations come.

For me this has happened not once but several times. Each time, I have had to make a choice whether I would give back to the Lord what was His or hang on tightly to what was comfortable and gave me a sense of identity. When we are doing something for the Lord, we feel wanted and needed and good about ourselves. Each time it took me much longer than it should have to open my hands and let go. I reasoned, argued, procrastinated, and tried to ignore the nudging that was telling me the Lord was moving and it was time to go. I knew if I gripped tightly that it would get ugly, but it was just so hard to let go and walk away. I don't want to be where the Lord is not, but I also like to be comfortable. Solitude and I don't get along very well! At one point the Lord said to me, "You would rather spend time with others than spend time alone with Me." He was right. It can be lonely waiting on the Lord. Sometimes He just wants me to be quiet and still, and stop the insanity long enough to hear His voice. There are times we need fellowship with others, and there are times we need to be alone with God. We can't pour from an empty cup.

So…here I am. I've passed the sagebrush and the oasis and even the cacti are beginning to get sparser and sparser. It's me and total quiet. The neighbors' tents have been out of sight for days, the ministries have faded into distant memories, the cell phone has lost reception; there is nothing but arid sand as far as my eyes can see. What now?

"Hello…God, are you there? There seems to have been a mistake. I think I took the wrong bus and got off at the wrong station. Do I continue to walk? Do I stop? Will I be here long? Where will my nourishment come from? Is this the end or the beginning? I don't know what to do! What? Is someone whispering to me? Could you talk louder, I'm not good at this whispering stuff. God, could you take pity on me and write a letter or call me or write some instructions in the sand so I know what to do? How long will I have to just be?"

Does anyone know what I'm talking about? This is where I'm at right now. I have picked up my tent and left my church home of twenty-seven years to follow the Lord to unknown places. I have picked up my tent and left a dearly loved fellowship group to follow the Lord to unknown places. I have picked up my tent and ended a ministry that the Lord blessed me with to follow Him to unknown places. I have picked up my tent and said goodbye to relationships to follow the Lord to unknown places. I have a dear friend who left a good job, home, and family to move across the country to follow the Lord to unknown places. She fed the homeless and became homeless herself. She held her hands open wide and literally gave the Lord everything! She had the clothes she was wearing and nothing else. Do you know what happens when we do this? First of all, this isn't for the faint of heart. Please know that the Lord doesn't ask everyone to do this. He never takes us on this journey unless we are willing. He is a gentleman and He will always ask if we are ready and willing to go to the deep end of the pool. If we say no, he will not push us off the diving board.

What happens when we say to God, "Anything, I will do anything I need to do to become more Christ-like"? It's not easy. We have to be more hungry for God than anything else, and we have to hunger and thirst for Him in a way that makes us do things we would never do if we weren't so desperate for more of Him. God does not strip us of ourselves to deny us. He strips us of ourselves so we can see Him with eyes that are clear and hearts that are free of everything that weighs us down. When we come to the end of ourselves, we finally allow God to be everything we need. He is our Daddy! He loves us deeper than any love we could ever imagine. He loves us to the point of death, and He loves us to the point of eternal life! When we open our hands and give back to Him everything He gave us in the first place, He upgrades. And when God upgrades, it's an upgrade! He doesn't skimp! My friend, who was formerly homeless, has the closest relationship with her Daddy than anyone I have ever known. She has so much faith and trust and never for a minute worried about her situation. She knows her Daddy will take care of her, and take care of her He has. The world is her oyster and the pearls are rolling in! She dared to pick up her tent and follow the Lord to unknown places and on the other side of her desert is an oasis full of blessings. In the stillness, she found her Daddy's heart. I know my travels in this desert will not last one minute longer than necessary to make me into the woman I was created to be, to claim my inheritance in all its fullness. I will be wiser and my senses will be keener. I will recognize more quickly the still small voice when I hear it, and I will have learned to be still and hear my Daddy's heart.

I don't know if you are in a desert right now, or an oasis, or somewhere in between. Maybe life is really going well for you, and you're on the fast track to promotion. Maybe you are waiting for promises that are too long in coming. Maybe you are home with babies and spend your days wiping peanut butter off your furniture. Maybe you are calling out to God that your life is a mess and you just don't think you can make it another day. We all have some stops on our journeys that we would just as soon not make. When your heart bleeds, your Father's heart bleeds. I do know that if you cry out to God He WILL answer you. You may or may not like the answer, but He will answer. You may have to make some changes in your life or you may have to gather every ounce of your courage and escape a toxic relationship. You may have to just cry out in total despair and say, "Jesus help me." That's all, just "Jesus help me."

We don't have to clean ourselves up before coming to Him. He will reach us where we are and pull us into Him and love us with a love that only He can. He doesn't care if we are dirty and covered in track marks, sell our bodies, drink too much or smoke like a chimney. HE LOVES US!!!!!!! He will clean us up. He just wants to hear His name on our lips and an invitation to be Lord of our life. If you can do nothing more than groan through your misery right now, be assured that your Father will hear your groans and come running. He's amazing that way. God created every one of us, and it is not His desire that anyone perish, not one single person. "The Lord is not slow in keeping His promise, as some understand slowness. He is patient with you, not wanting anyone to perish, but everyone to come to repentance," 2 Peter 3:9. He wants to gather us like little chicks under His wings and protect us with the fierceness of a mama bear.

Lay it down. That's the name of this chapter. If there is anything in your life that sticks to your hands like paste to a kindergartener, you may need to lay it down. I'm not saying God won't give it back, but He just wants to know that it's not more important to you than He is. If you can truly pry yourself off any "idol" in your life and open those sticky hands up wide then you are probably safe. He doesn't want your things; He just wants you. He is a jealous God and wants all of you, not just a leftover now and then or a crumb when you have extra. Despite my shortcomings, one thing I have is an unshakable trust in my Daddy; I tell Him that almost every day. I may not know how long I will be in this desert or what the next step is. I may not know when the bus will come pick me up and take me back to civilization, but I know that all I have given up will be restored many times over.

Even in this arid place I am blessed beyond what I could ask or imagine. Every single day my Daddy makes sure I have provision for the day ahead. He blesses me with summer rain and sunshine and a respite from the long cold winter months. The flowers are in full bloom, the foxes in our shed are growing up, Jake is learning where his potty is, and, most of all, I have an amazing family and friends that love me. Sometimes life is hard, and sometimes life is good, but always God is in control! I am a mother, and my mother's heart wants to grab you and hug you and make it all better and hide you from harm – truly I do. Even though that is not possible, I know Someone who can! We may have to endure trials here but our Father's arms will be forever around us and one day, if we have confessed Him as Lord of our life, we will be with Him in His home where every tear will be wiped away and we will never again have pain or struggles. "He will wipe away every tear from their eyes. There will be no more death or mourning or crying or pain, for the old order of things has passed away," Revelation 21:4.

While I'm here, I want to love the very best I can and give of myself like there is an endless supply. But when my time is up, I am so out of here. Party at Jesus' house! I am only passing through, and I confess I am homesick. I know I am with my Father now because He is in me. "We know that we live in Him and He in us, because He has given us of His Spirit," 1 John 4:13. But, for now, I live in an imperfect world and it is not pain-free. It is by His Spirit in me that I can endure and overcome. Someday, I'm going to live in His perfect world. You and I will have some crazy times together! For now, let's lay it all down together and keep our eyes on the goal ahead.

14

Potato Fights & Squirt Guns

I don't know you but I think I would like you if we met. I'm pretty sure we could share some chocolate and laughs and be friends. I love spending time with family and friends, and new brothers and sisters. Sometimes I like just being quiet together while listening to the birds as a gentle breeze blows on our faces. I love listening to children laugh, little girls in sun dresses, and little boys in overalls. I don't take myself too seriously and can laugh at myself easily. Sometimes I'm the only one in on the joke but that's ok.

Right now I'm thinking about our friend Martha again. Would you humor me and take a peek into her kitchen with me? Martha is busy and more than a little miffed at her sister. Does anyone besides me see the need to lighten the mood a little? I think Jesus has a sense of humor and wouldn't mind too much if we threw a little laughter into the kitchen scenario. Now, if I were there right about the time Martha was making the gravy, I would grab a handful of flour and throw it at her. If you are gasping at the inappropriateness of it all, then you definitely take yourself too seriously. I'm sure Martha wouldn't find it exactly hilarious either, but people, we need to lighten up! Could it be that Jesus might have even caught Himself smiling? I'm not trying to show disrespect to Him, I can be quite reverent, but I just think Martha was wound a bit too tight. More often than not, I have been like her, but with age comes a little unwinding. We learn to relax a bit, probably because we're too tired anymore to sweat the small stuff. Nowadays, just thinking about sweating the small stuff calls for a nap to recover!

Can I Just be Real?

I wish you would have been seated at my table when a mashed potato fight broke out right there in the dining room. You would have loved it. My husband was gone (of course, he's the sensible one!) and I had a house full of teenagers. I was entertaining them with the story of when I was growing up, if someone said, "throw me a biscuit" or a potato, or whatever, they'd better be ready to catch it because it would be literally thrown and not passed like civilized people. The kids listened to the story and were so well-behaved that it got the best of me. Obviously they were from civilized families (until they came to our house). With a straight face right in the middle of conversation I quietly grabbed a handful of mashed potatoes (no gravy) and slung them at the nice young man across the table from me hitting him square in the chest. My table full of teenagers sat in stunned silence with mouths gaping open…for about ten seconds. And then the potatoes flew! Brace yourself for this. They flew on the ceiling, the curtains, the walls, and the floor, everywhere! It was madness, and it was fun! Yes, we all cleaned it up together, but even weeks later I would find stray potatoes on the ceiling or still clinging to a curtain. Can you just see Martha right now? She seriously would need CPR! We also have been known to have mashed potato sculpting contests, culminating into some great big awesome potato slinging.

One of my favorite memories is when I was with the church ladies painting steps and railings at the camp we sponsored. (I'm already laughing so hard I'm snorting!) I was working next to a very prim-appearing lady. We were giggling about putting paint hand prints on somebody's butt. She, yes she, began egging me on and daring me to do it (honestly, it was all her). I asked her how attached she was to the jeans she was wearing, and she informed me she got them at a thrift store and was not very attached. Well, good grief, what else was I supposed to do? I didn't need a written invitation when she bent over! I promptly dipped my hands in the paint tray and slapped both open hands square on her backside with a little more force than I had anticipated. She almost fell over face-first, and for a moment I thought I had gone too far. The church ladies gasped in unison, marched over to her to make sure she was all right, and then marched over to me and proceeded to reprimand me like I had committed the unforgiveable sin! Oh dear one, it was all I could do to keep a straight face and act properly scorned. Obviously, I was the only one with a sense of humor! The lady whose butt I painted? She acted very proper until we were out of sight of the other ladies, and then we both rolled with laughter. Please don't dare me to do something; I have not been known to have a lot of restraint. Oddly enough, that was the last time I was invited to help paint and whenever I appeared on work day, I was watched very carefully.

If you think I'm totally crazy you are pretty observant. Of course I am! I'm crazy about God, my family, my friends, and I'm crazy about enjoying life. I won't lie; years of struggling with anxiety, depression and painful illnesses have taken a lot out of me. It's taken its toll and stolen a lot of my joy and energy. I have been delivered from the bondages of anxiety and depression straight from the pit of hell, but I'm still learning to walk out of my chains. They have been broken, and I'm no longer a prisoner, but I'm still "renewing my mind" and training my body to react differently when fear creeps in like a stalker in the dark. I still struggle with anxiety and I strongly dislike getting in a car and going farther than a couple miles. The enclosed space is not my friend! This presents some challenges when you live in a town with one stoplight, one grocery store and the nearest Walmart is twenty miles away.

Years ago I had to get on an airplane. I spent the night before in a fetal position on my couch sobbing and begging not to go. I realize that for most of you this is completely irrational, and it is. If you enjoy traveling you probably can't imagine what is wrong with me. Fear is not rational, and it is not from God! So we do what we have to do – we overcome. Not only did I get on that airplane and fly across the country, but then I rode in a U-Haul for several days back home. The Lord is my strength, and together we made it.

Why am I telling you this? Because satan has stolen from me years of health, peace, and joy, and not only do I want my life back, but I want your life back! If you have never had the enemy steal from you, then put this book down right now and thank God. You are one of the few and lucky. The rest of us can and will stand tall and straight, and take back everything that is ours, and then for good measure, we will pillage the camp of the enemy. Our tongue holds the power of blessing and cursing. "Out of the same mouth comes praise and cursing," James 3:10. We have been given authority from our Heavenly Father to speak blessing over our life. We are able to speak life-giving scripture over our bondages in Jesus name, and the chains HAVE to fall off. "Greater is He that is in us [Christ] than he [satan] that is in the world," 1 John 4:4. We are overcomers! It is important for so many reasons, including our healing, to find scriptures that encourage us and speak strength into us and speak them out loud over and over all day long. God's words hold power and authority and when we speak them we are claiming our victory over those powers of darkness, stomping the enemy into the ground, and glorifying our Heavenly Father. We are victors, NOT victims, sweet friend. Get your roar on! At the end of this book I have given you some scriptures that speak clearly of who we are in Christ. Please take what speaks to your heart or find your own and use them as your sword. I have also supplied a "Prayer of Authority" for you to speak out if you wish.

We have a choice: we can wear our past wounds as a badge of honor and talk about them to anyone who will listen, or we can make a daily choice to be overcomers. Overcoming does not mean denying our wounds. However, it does mean we no longer allow them to define who we are. It means not dredging up the past and camping there. That gives satan too much power over us. My wounds still hurt, and my heart is still tender. I don't easily trust, and even though I am trying to be more transparent, my trust has to be earned. The Lord has blessed me with some amazing people who take great care with my heart and treat it tenderly. For that I am grateful. You need to find those people in your life also and hang onto them tightly.

So, yes, I have potato fights, bring home puppies who stain my carpet, and am not to be trusted if you turn your back on me. I laugh until I snort, and ride a motorcycle without a helmet. But here's the thing: I have spent two-thirds of my life battling depression, anxiety, migraine headaches, and fear. I have been in more hospitals than most of you will ever be in your lifetime. I have had more needles in me than a well-used pin cushion.

I lost my earthly father to a heart attack. I lost my mother to a ten-year battle with kidney failure and heart disease. I lost my mother-in-law to Alzheimer's, my father-in-law to a prolonged illness, my grandmother, sister-in-law and niece to cancer, a sister-in-law to epilepsy, a brother-in-law to diabetes, my grandfather to an aneurysm, an aunt to kidney failure, and an uncle to a heart attack. I went to five family funerals in one year. The doctors would say my family history doesn't look promising, but I say, "I am a child of the King and my DNA is His." I have made a choice to live and not die (until the Lord says it's time). I will no longer be a victim to the devil! I know who my Daddy is, and I know how to fight. I believe in Jesus for my healing. However, I still battle anxiety almost daily. I have stomach pain. I will more than likely have to change my entire life-style and eating patterns. Whether God heals me here on earth or in heaven, I refuse to give up! Learning to fight hard and trust Jesus has made me who I am today.

We can't be giant slayers if we have no giant to slay! I purpose to make the enemy miserable as I praise God in the midst of the storm. I have to choose daily to not allow myself a victim mentality. Some days I'm successful, and some days I'm not. I get tired of missing out on life events as I have to stay home so often because of illness. But, I spend those times I'm confined in sweet fellowship with my Daddy. I worship through the pain. I share with Him the brokenness of my heart and the sorrow of, once again, not being able to live life as others do. I lament and remind God that "iron sharpens iron" and I need some "iron" in my life. I need to be able to leave my yard and have fun and carelessly laugh while enjoying something besides the walls of my home. Occasionally I get to do that. But, in His grace, He has given me friends and family who will come to my home and do life with me. They bring me food, watch movies with me, remind me endlessly how much they love me and how awesome I am, cheer for me, accept me as I am, hope and dream with me, and push me when I need a push. I know it won't always be this way because God has promised my healing, and I have a destiny yet to be fulfilled.

I make no apologies for playing hard and crying hard. I will have potato fights and throw flour and shoot squirt guns and laugh at silly movies. I have seen the ravages of illness and death, and I'm sure I will again. We live in a broken world, and it happens. But I am a warrior now; I know the end of the story: God wins! Actually, God has already won long ago, and I remind myself daily that I have the mind of Christ. His mind does not fear and is not anxious. His mind loves and laughs and embraces the day with confidence. (As I said, I am still a work in progress in these areas, but I take it one day at a time. My mind has had a lot of years of having its own way. It's a bit stubborn!)

I have given my friends permission to call me anytime and by anytime I mean the middle of the night if necessary.

Some of them have taken me up on the offer, and I love those middle of the night calls. Why? If you knew me, you would know how dearly I love my sleep so it's not because of insomnia. It's because satan doesn't work from 9-5 and then call it a day and go home. He's no fool! What better time to prowl (our enemy prowls like a roaring lion) than under the cover of darkness. He's kind of creepy that way! What better time to turn on the light (you know, your spiritual floodlight) than, yep, you guessed it, in the dark! When a brother or sister is coming under attack and is struggling, we need to get our prayer on and start doing some damage. I have seen some of the greatest breakthroughs at 3:00 a.m. I just heard this analogy and I like it: The stars are always in the sky, but we only see them at night because their light shines brightest in the darkness!

Please know how totally precious you are to your heavenly Father and how crazy mad in love with you He is. Together we will get through this, and you better be ready because when we get to heaven I'm going to give you a bear hug you won't soon forget. You might want to watch your back because I may be hiding a squirt gun or a handful of mashed potatoes behind mine!

15
One Last Cup of Tea

Dear friend, I think we are coming to an end of our time together. I feel a bit sad because in some crazy way I feel like I am just getting to know you, and I want to linger a while longer. I don't want to be in a hurry as we explore God together. I want our time to be sweet, meaningful, and comfortable like old friends in front of a fireplace with a mug of warm tea. None of us are really very different; we all desire love and intimacy, and to be needed and wanted. We bleed when wounded and cry when hurt. We laugh when we feel joy and can't help but giggle when someone has paint handprints on their butt. We were all formed in the womb by an insanely loving Father, and we all want to be loved. We are family!

I have known wounds, and I have known healing. It is my deepest prayer that you too will know healing from your wounds. I so desperately hate evil and rarely allow myself to dwell on all the abuse and horrors in this world because my heart feels like it will die if I do. With everything in me, I want to walk with every brother and sister into their freedom. I want to gather all the hurting souls into my arms to hug and soothe away all the pain. I'm sure that's how God feels times a zillion! How He must hurt when we hurt. My heart and mind aren't nearly big enough to fathom His love and compassion. Someday when we meet face-to-face I just want to fall at His feet and soak in His glory and love (we can do that now but it will be even sweeter when we are face-to-face).

I wish I could tell you that I have it all together and every day I go to my prayer closet and pray wonderful prayers. I wish I could say I worship every day and have meaningful devotionals and never sin. But I am just like you. Some days

I feel so close to God. Some days I feel far away from Him. But I want to be close to Him every day, to be faithful and purposeful in my relationship with Him. I am saved by grace and am a work in progress. I love my heavenly Daddy so dearly and trust Him with all of me. I want to want nothing of this world and everything of Him. May you draw near to your heavenly Father and allow Him to show you the way He sees you and not the distorted view of yourself you see in the mirror. God says, "For my yoke is easy and my burden is light," Matthew 11:30. Yet, we are so hard on ourselves. We believe the lies the world has handed us on a silver platter. It's convinced us of all the "important" things we simply cannot live without. Please believe how precious you are! God looks at our hearts. Give your heart to Him and let Him bring healing and peace and mend its brokenness.

May you make time to sit at His feet, to cease striving and running around, and simply be with your Father. Put down the dish towels, and let Jesus' laughter fill your heart with a new song. I may lament at times about my lack of mobility in this season of my life, but, the truth is, it has forced me to press in to God in ways that I never would have done on my own. I am not sorry that I have had this time to sit at His feet and get to know Him up close and personal. It is a blessing! It has taught me things that I could never have learned no matter how many conferences I would have gone to. There is something about being vulnerable and weak that draws Him near. He is all I need. I love sitting at His feet and learning His heart. He is my strength and He is my joy!

You are loved. You are precious. Today is a new day, so leave the past on yesterday's doorstep and start fresh.

I pray for you right now. I pray you will shine with the glory of the One living inside you. I pray you will be undone at the wonder of your Daddy. I pray every day you will experience a new revelation of who He is and who you are in Him. Rise and shine beautiful one. Rise and Shine!

Bless you, my new friend. Jesus loves you, and so do I!

Epilogue

Dear one, you have and are ALL things because Christ lives in you! You have power, authority, peace and love. No matter who you are or what you've done, if you have received Christ, you are redeemed and forgiven! You are not condemned, disgraced or forgotten! There is only One Judge, and He judges through eyes of love and compassion.

If you have not yet allowed Christ to love your heart and are angry with believers because they have judged or condemned you, please try to forgive and understand that a believer in Christ is just a sinner saved by grace, and sometimes we forget how far we too have fallen. We are all children, created by a loving Father, and we are on this earth for only a short time. Let's lay down our swords against each other and stop tearing one another to pieces.

"Our struggle is NOT against flesh and blood, but against the rulers, against the authorities, against the powers of this dark world and against the spiritual forces of evil in the heavenly realms," Ephesians 6:12. Our fight is against satan and NOT our brother or sister, friend or spouse. Satan is the one who causes division and strife, hatred and jealousy, envy and arrogance, pride, and stubborn hearts. If we believe his lies, we become hateful, and full of condemnation. Let's get our eyes off of others, get on our knees, and seek the heart of our Father. Once you get a glimpse of your Father's heart, the only thing you will be able to do is stare at Him in awe. When His Glory hits you, you will be undone! He will touch any anger, hate, condemnation, jealousy, or pain in your heart, and you will never look at Him or others or yourself the same. NEVER!

So cry out to Jesus. Are you scared? Are you too busy? Are you too stubborn? Are you just too convinced that He's not real? Then I especially dare you to cry out to Him. If He's not real, then you have nothing to lose. If you would rather hold on to your stubbornness, anger, unforgiveness, or whatever it is keeping you from Him, then you have everything to lose! One day you and I will stand before Him, and even though God is loving and compassionate, He is also fair. If you reject Him, He will have no choice but to reject you. "Whoever acknowledges me before men, I will acknowledge him before my Father in heaven. But whoever disowns me before men, I will disown him before my Father in heaven," Matthew 10:32-33. He pushes Himself on no one and will never force us to love Him. He did not create a world full of robots! Would you want someone to love you because they had to? That's NOT love! If you are reading this and are mad at God, don't think He truly exists, or are hurting and full of bitterness, then I plead with you to give Him a chance. See if He won't bend His ear when you cry to Him and show you just how real He is. He promises that those who seek Him will find Him. Take Him up on that promise!

If you don't know Jesus, I will show you just how easy it is. You may think it is too complicated, or have to "have it all together" first. You come to Jesus as you are. Salvation and forgiveness of sins is not about working for it or earning it. It is about accepting Jesus as our Savior and receiving what He has already done for us. Let me walk you through it.

"Righteousness from God comes through faith in Jesus Christ to all who believe. There is no difference, for all have sinned and fall short of the glory of God," Romans 3:23.

"God demonstrates His own love for us in this: While we were still sinners, Christ died for us," Romans 5:8.

"If you confess with your mouth, 'Jesus is Lord,' and believe in your heart that God raised Him from the dead, you will be saved," Romans 10:9.

"Everyone who calls on the name of the Lord will be saved," Romans 10:13.

Pretty simple, isn't it? All you have to do is ask Jesus to be your Savior, believe that He is the Son of God, and that He died and was raised from the dead so that you can have eternal life. You can do this right now all by yourself if you wish. I will walk you through a prayer:

"Jesus, I ask you to come into my heart and cleanse me from all sin. I give you permission to be Lord of my life. I believe you died on the cross because you love me. I believe you rose again and You are the Son of God. I want to spend eternity with You. I give You my heart. In Jesus' name. Amen."

Congratulations! You are now a new creation. Once you have accepted the gift of Jesus, He will lead, and guide you. I recommend that you connect with other believers so that you can begin your journey with solid teaching and training. They will come alongside you and help you grow. If you don't have a Bible, ask a solid believer to help you get one. Begin to read God's word and ask Him to help you understand what you are reading. As I said, He loves to talk to you and is overjoyed to walk beside you as you experience your own journey into intimacy with Him.

If you would like to talk with me or obtain a copy of this book for a friend, you can email me at: bljreal@gmail.com

Who You Are In Christ

I am God's temple and His spirit lives in me	*1 Cor 3:16 & 2 Cor 6:16*
I have the same Spirit in me that raised Christ from the dead	*Rom 8:11*
I have the mind of Christ	*1 Cor 2:16*
I have God's power at work in me and through me	*Eph 3:10*
I have the wisdom of God	*James 1:5*
I have the Spirit of Truth in me	*John 16:13*
I have been given eternal life and nothing can snatch me from the Father	*John 10:28, 29*
I have been established, anointed and sealed by God	*Col 3:3*
I have been forgiven of all my sins and healed of all my diseases	*Psalm 103:3*
I have been redeemed from the pit	*Psalm 103:4*
I am taught deep & hidden things by His Spirit	*1 Cor 2:10*
I have the power to demolish strongholds	*2 Cor 10:4*

I have His Spirit in
me testifying that I am
His child and am controlled
by the Spirit of God
living within me .... *Rom 8:6 & Rom 8:9*

I am raised with
Christ and seated in
the heavenly realms .... *Eph 2:6*

I can take every
thought captive and make
it obedient to Christ .... *2 Cor 10:5*

I am strengthened
and protected from
the evil one .... *2 Thess 3:3*

I have God's
ministering Spirit in me .... *Heb 1:14*

I have God's streams
of living water flowing
from me .... *John 7:38*

I am witness that
the prince of this world
stands condemned .... *John 16:11*

I have authority to
speak to my mountains
and they will move .... *Matt 17:20, 21*

I have not been given
a spirit of fear but of power,
love, a sound mind,
discipline and self-control .... *2 Tim 1:7*

I am transformed by
the renewing of my mind
and I will no longer
conform to this world .... *Rom 12:2*

I overflow with hope
by the power of the
Holy Spirit as I trust in God................................Rom 15:13

I live by faith
not by sight...2 Cor 5:7

I am Christ's
ambassador...2 Cor 5:20

I am compelled by
Christ's love..2 Cor 5:14

I have divine powers
to demolish all
strongholds and
take captive every
thought to make it
obedient to Christ..2 Cor 10:4, 5

I live by the Spirit .... Gal 5:25

I have been chosen
before the creation of
the world to be blameless
and holy in the sight
of God and to His glory ....Eph 1:4

I am no longer an infant
tossed back and forth by the
waves of every teaching,
but have become mature in the
knowledge of the fullness
of Christ ....Phil 4:13, 14

I am strong in the Lord...Eph 6:10

I will be anxious for nothing................................Phil 1:4

I can do all things
through Christ ....Eph 4:13

I have been rescued from
darkness, redeemed and
bought through Christ's
great mercy... Col 1:13

I labor with Christ's
energy (not my own)
which powerfully
works in me... *Col 1:29*

I am in Christ, therefore
the powers of darkness
have been disarmed,
been made a public spectacle
and have been triumphed
over by the work of the cross................................. *Col 2:15*

I have been covered by
the blood of Jesus and will
draw near to God with
a sincere heart in full
assurance of faith that
I have been cleansed
and made pure and stand
in NO condemnation before Him........................... *Rom 8:1*

I am clear-minded and
self-controlled through the
power of the Holy Spirit .... *1 Peter 4:6*

I have no need to fear,
I will not be shaken, my heart
is steadfast and secure
because I trust in the Lord
and in the end He will
triumph over my enemies............................. *Psalm 112:6-8*

I have been forgiven of
all my sins and healed of
all my diseases. Christ has
redeemed my life from the
pit and will satisfy my
desires with all good things......................... *Psalm 103:3-7*

I have been given authority
to trample snakes and
scorpions and overcome
all the power of darkness
and nothing will harm me .... *Luke 10:19*

Prayer of Authority

Heavenly Father, I give you control of my mind, emotions, will, and body. I invite you to be Lord of my life and give you complete control in the name of Jesus Christ.

I put on the full armor: the belt of truth, the breastplate of righteousness, the shield of faith, the helmet of salvation, the shoes of the Gospel, and the sword of the Spirit. With this armor fully in place, I will war against the principalities of darkness with the power and authority of the Lord Jesus Christ.

Satan, I bind you. You have no control over my intellect, my mind, my emotions, my will or my body. I loose myself from every stronghold and all bondage in the name of the Lord Jesus Christ. Jesus has taken victory over you on the cross, and you have no power over my life in any way. I command every stronghold to bend its knee to the authority of Jesus Christ and all truth in Him. You are not allowed to speak to me or place any assignments over me or my household.

Thank you, Lord, that the devil is a powerless, defeated foe and that in You, I am victorious over him. Thank you that your angels stand guard over me and my household day and night and no power of darkness shall ever overtake me. Thank you, Father, that I have the mind of Christ and that the same Spirit that raised Jesus from the dead is the same Spirit that lives in me.

Father, search my heart and know me; create in me a clean heart and keep me from willful sin, for it is You that my heart seeks and You that I long to glorify all the days of my life.

In Jesus Name,
Amen and Amen

Endnotes

All scripture is quoted from Zondervan NIV Study Bible unless otherwise stated.

[1] Love and Respect by Emerson Eggerich, Copyright 2004, Thomas Nelson Publishing

[2] Anything by Jennie Allen, Copyright 2011, Thomas Nelson Publishing

[3] Oswald Chambers in Not Knowing Whither from the Quotable Oswald Chambers. Copyright 2008, Oswald Chambers Publications Association, Ltd., Discovery House Publishers